Hidden Charms 3
Transactions of the conference 2021

Edited by Jeremy Harte and Brian Hoggard

Apotropaios Publications

Cover image: Antique dowry chest from Indian subcontinent from Brian Hoggard's collection

Hidden Charms 3
Transactions of the Hidden Charms conference 2021
© The Authors 2023

Published by Apotropaios Publications, 2023

ISBN 978-1-3999-4868-5

Printed in England

All rights reserved. No part of this publication may be reproduced, stored in a retrieval system, or transmitted, in any form or by any means without the permission of the author and publisher.

www.apotropaios.co.uk

Contents

Introduction
    Brian Hoggard   3

Lectures

Horse skulls and their use in magic
    Brian Hoggard   5

Rethinking the perception of magic and rituals in archaeological contexts and in material culture: A three-fold dialogue between field archaeologists, academics, and the public
    Debora Moretti   13

Arrow sharpening marks: An English church myth
    Jeremy Harte   25

Hiding in plain sight: Pagan protection rituals in popular celebrations of St Brigid in Ireland
    Jeannine Woods   41

Circles and a square: Magical protection at the Maison Forte de Reignac, a fortified dwelling in the Dordogne region of France
    Linda Wilson   57

X marks the post: The use of the X as an apotropaic symbol
    Chris Wood   69

Witchcraft and counter-magic in early twentieth-century Cornwall
    Jason Semmens   85

Apotropaic traces on building components: Beyond function and decoration
    Marc Robben   89

Tower of strength: Buildings archaeology and apotropaic symbols in medieval elite society
    James Wright   101

Poster Presentations

Where there's muck, there's magic: Recording meaningful marks in Peak District farm buildings
 Andy Bentham   113

Merels: Games, graffiti, symbols
 Anthea Hawdon   123

Notre Dame de Temniac: The landscape of a nineteenth-century altar back
 Linda Wilson   127

About the authors   135

Index   137

Introduction

Brian Hoggard

Having been rescheduled twice due to covid the Hidden Charms 3 conference took place on Saturday 2nd October 2021 at St Mary's Creative Space in Chester. St Mary's is a beautiful church with lots of interesting features including fine roof bosses, grotesques which include a mermaid, several memento mori and at least one deliberate burn mark on the tower door. Into this space we filed ready for a day of interesting lectures covering various angles and approaches to the topic of magical building protection.

The conference was a nice mix of spoken presentations and posters which provided much stimulus for conversation in the breaks. As at Hidden Charms 2 which happened in Salisbury in 2018 we had representation from The Folklore Society and Raking Light who were happy to chat and provide information also. The City of Chester itself has many fascinating architectural features which all helped to make the weekend really fun, interesting and fuelled with beer in the evenings.

It is clear that the subject of magical house protection is becoming far more widely considered than it was when I first embarked on my own research project back in 1999. There are now many more people doing research in many countries across the world and we are all gradually connecting with each-other, learning from each-other and increasingly working together. I would like to think that the community around the Hidden Charms conferences has played a big part in that.

The world of academia is an interesting one with much fascinating work going but there are always sharks swimming in those waters and those people have also made their presence felt over the years since our first conference. I feel confident that we tend to attract the good people to our events, people who approach the subject in a mutually supportive way, instead of those who are acquisitive and out for personal gain.

My own book on the subject made it into paperback during 2020 so I have had a busy time doing lots of lectures supporting that, spreading the word about the subject and hopefully explaining how much more there is still to discover.

Our friend and colleague John Billingsley stepped away from being one of the organisers for HC3, being very busy with several other projects, but he will still be a presence at the conferences I'm sure.

Hidden Charms 4 is set to take place in York on 15th April 2023 at the

National Centre for Early Music. It promises to be a fantastic weekend with many interesting lectures. There is every intention for there to be a 5th conference, location currently being considered...

Horse Skulls and their Use in Magic

Brian Hoggard

Horse skulls have been recovered from many old buildings during demolition, alteration or repair. It is clear that these impressive skulls, like many other deliberately concealed items, were placed within the fabric of the building for magical protection. They have also been found beneath buildings, suggesting something along the lines of a foundation sacrifice. They have been found throughout Europe, Scandinavia, Russia and the USA and it is likely that the practice of concealing them in this way had an even greater geographic spread. There are many beliefs and legends about horses stretching back as far as humans have interacted with them. There are also folk dances which heavily involve horse skulls or substitutes for them such as the Mari Lwyd and Hooden Horse. Add to this the luck associated with horseshoes and we have a potent mixture of beliefs and practices connected with the horse.

I have written about horse skulls before.[1] This paper will develop these works with new material looking at the physical evidence recovered from buildings, and with reference to other practices.

Investigation into the meaning of concealed horse skulls has been going on since the mid twentieth century. In that era, there were two favoured explanations; the acoustic theory and the theory of foundation sacrifice. The real answer appears to be a bit less binary and other beliefs about the nature of the horse may be at play.

The acoustic theory is built upon the testimony of people who said this was why horse skulls were concealed. Albert Sandklef in his 1949 paper, dealing with Swedish examples found beneath threshing barns, was told that the presence of the horse skulls beneath the floor enhanced the sound of the flails during threshing, making a more pleasant ringing sound.[2] Similarly, Sean Ó Súilleabháin in his 1945 paper for the Society of Antiquaries of Ireland found some cottage owners claiming that the presence of the horse skull beneath a stone in front of the fireplace made the dancing sound better.[3] In England the explanation for the presence of 24 horse skulls screwed to the underside of the floor in the pub called The Portway at Staunton-on-Wye in Herefordshire was that it 'made the fiddle go better'.[4] This may have been the accepted explanation by the people spoken to at the time but there are some problems with the theory.

Why use horse skulls to amplify acoustics rather than some other resonator? Assuming there was a ready supply of clean, de-fleshed horse skulls, why would these be preferred for enhancing sound? Was it simply the quantity of them available as raw material from neighbouring knacker's yards? It would be strange if these yards had gone to the trouble of stripping and cleaning all of these skulls on the off-chance that a local builder needed some to enhance acoustics, and even stranger that this became a practice over such a wide geographical area. I have not conducted scientific tests on the resonance of horse skulls but as a musician who owns an antique horse skull I can confirm that there is no acoustic enhancement in the immediate vicinity when I play next to mine. Perhaps it needs to be bolted to a piece of timber for any effect.

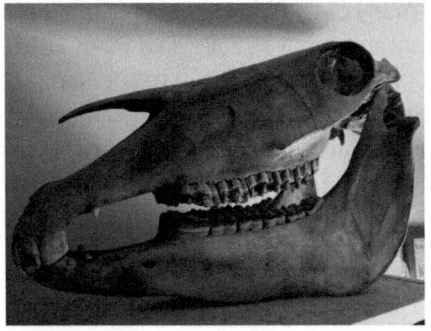

Fig. 1. *An antique horse skull.*

Horse skulls are quite large and would have attracted attention being collected and interred in a building. This suggests that the acoustic theory provided a plausible explanation rather than a factual reason. It may be that this excuse was deployed so often that people who did not know the real reason for their use came to believe the excuse instead. The amount of effort invested by the builders of The Portway in screwing 24 horse skulls to the underside of the floor seems out of proportion to the acoustic benefit expected from it. Another example from Bungay in Suffolk was discovered in the 1930s where on lifting two of the floorboards, 'beneath the joists were rows of horse skulls, laid with great regularity, the incisor teeth of each resting on a square of oak or stone ... The [floor] boards, which were of red pine, rested immediately upon the skulls'. The room contained up to forty horse skulls, each 'carefully prepared and boiled, and ... placed in position with great care and accuracy'. The adjoining house also revealed several horse skulls under the floor but these had been removed.[5] There must surely have been better ways to improve acoustics – ways which were far less likely to arouse suspicions of superstitious behaviour.

At Elsdon in Northumberland three horse skulls were discovered in the bell-turret of the church; these are now on display in the church as part of an exhibition. This suggests that horse skulls and bells may have related functions. One of the roles of the church bell is scare away evil spirits – perhaps the horse skulls were placed in the belief that they might enhance the sound of the bells but also assist in warding off evil.

Many concealed horse skulls were set into places where they are unlikely to have served as good conductors and amplifiers of sound. Four were 'found beneath the doorway of a home in the fourteenth-century deserted mediaeval village at Thuxton, Norfolk'.[6] Another was discovered in a house known as Squeen Lodge at Ballaugh, Isle of Man. 'While the builders were removing the first floor joists they uncovered what appeared to be a skull and hip bone set into a joist hole ... [on investigation] ... it was in fact a horse's skull with twin boar tusks inserted into the tooth sockets of the upper jaw.' The find is thought to be of the eighteenth century.[7] At a cottage on Quickwell Hill in St David's, Pembrokeshire, former resident Robin Oakley reported that a horse skull is on display in a case which was reputedly discovered in foundations during renovations. At Halton East, North Yorkshire, horse skulls were discovered beneath the flagstones of a cottage during restoration.[8] Excavations at Hornby Castle in Wensleydale revealed a horse head buried within an early fourteenth century wall. Correspondent Rubyna Matthews reported in November 2013:

> I am the Field Officer of the Architectural and Archaeological Society of Durham and Northumberland and since 2010 we have been undertaking a programme of fieldwork, mainly comprising excavation on a site within the grounds of Hornby Castle in Wensleydale North Yorkshire. The site comprises a 'pleasaunce' or detached structure for the entertainment of important guests of the owners in the 14th and 15th Centuries, a branch of the Nevilles and later the Conyers family. During Season 3 (2012) much to our surprise we uncovered a horse's head that had been deliberately buried within the core of a wall of early 14th Century date. The horse had been decapitated below the third vertebrae.[9]

There are plenty more examples where the acoustic theory clearly does not apply. In the USA four horse skulls were found in the Jarrot Mansion at the Cahokia Courthouse Historic State site, one in a cavity right beside the fireplace, the others under the floor. The building was constructed for French settlers by English Americans in the late eighteenth century. The practice of concealing horse skulls goes back at least to the sixteenth century in Portmarnock, Ireland, where one was found beneath the floor during an excavation and another eight grouped together beneath another.[10]
Sonja Hukantaival reports that in Finland horse skulls are traditionally said to have been concealed within the hearth to ward off pests. She says:

> Even though horse skulls are often mentioned in the folklore, there

are few documented finds of concealed horse skulls in Finland. Still, it has been pointed out that in some areas finding a horse skull in an old hearth when demolishing it is very common. Perhaps a bit too common, since people do not think that it is something they should report to the local museum. Only remarkable finds tend to get reported; this is evident in two cases where the complete skeleton of a horse was found in the hearth foundation.[11]

Placing skulls in hearths implies a more general form of protection from evil, as the hearth is always open to the sky and hence more vulnerable to attack than other areas of a property.

Other writers have suggested that the practice of concealing horse skulls is more related to foundation sacrifice. Eurwyn Wiliam, for example, cites 27 examples in his study of horse skulls in Wales and concludes that protection was the key purpose and that the practice was more likely to be related to foundation sacrifice.[12] Foundation sacrifice is the practice of making an offering to the site of a building, or the building itself, so that it won't later take a life. This idea is extremely ancient, has been practised all over the world, and still happens today. Not long ago a video of this happening in Albania was shown to be me where a goat had its throat cut over the foundations before a second pour of concrete was about to happen. Such a belief cannot be discounted in Britain and horse skulls have certainly been deposited in the foundations of buildings, but for the skull to be available for use in a foundation the horse must have been killed elsewhere and its head detached from its body before foundations were laid. Strictly speaking this makes it a foundation deposit, not sacrifice.

There are many bits of folklore and material evidence to suggest that horse skulls bring luck and ward off evil; they are often included in or near hearths which implies a protective function. One of the best examples comes from Enid Porter's *Cambridgeshire Customs and Folklore*:

> W.H. Barrett recalls that his uncle, a builder, secured the contract in 1897 for erecting a Primitive Methodist Chapel at Black Horse Drove. One day he sent his nephew, then aged 6, with his elder brother to the knacker's yard to buy a horse's head. When the two boys returned with it they watched the workmen dig the trench for the foundations and then saw their uncle carefully mark the centre of the site by driving into the ground a wooden stake. The men gathered round while the uncle uncorked a bottle of beer, then the horse's head was placed in the bottom of the trench, the first glass of liquor

poured from the bottle was thrown on to it and, when the rest of the beer had been drunk, the men shovelled bricks and mortar on the top of the head. It was explained to W.H. Barrett that this was an old heathen custom to drive evil and witchcraft away.[13]

The custom of concealing horse skulls apparently continued until at least the early nineteenth century in Armagh, Northern Ireland, where '*the frontal bones of a horse's head were regarded as being particularly sonsie (lucky), and were often buried in barn floors and under the thresholds of dwelling houses for this reason*'.[14] In several of the Welsh examples skulls were clearly believed to protect properties against evil and witchcraft, with some from church roofs thought to 'dispel the spirits'.[15]

To these examples we must also add those from Scandinavia and Russia, where there appears to have been a belief that horse skulls could keep away pests and evil. An example, used to protect bees, is in the Ethnographic Museum in St Petersberg. Adina Hulubas from the Romanian Academy told me that horse skulls are placed in orchards there to ward off evil.

In the Bryant Homestead, a 1776 house in South Deerfield, Massachussets, a horse skull was discovered in a thick wall near the chimney. The finders, Rocky and Kathy Foley, reported that when they removed it from the wall they discovered a piece of paper in the eye socket reading, 'Colonel David M. Bryant and Family took possession of this farm on April 29, 1848'; the note also listed the names of his wife and six children.[16] Evidently the horse skull was supposed to protect those named in the letter.

Bryn Ellis' *Halkyn Mountain Communities in Times Past* includes a picture of horse skulls in its account of a 1726 house called Lygan y Wern. The skulls, one black and one bleached white, were found in October 1965 during floor repairs in one of the front rooms. A local researcher named Garfield Bagshaw interpreted the two skulls as meaning that the unbleached one was set into the earth to 'propitiate the spirits of the soil, which had been disturbed to build the house', and the bleached one was there to prevent evil from entering. The skulls were apparently replaced afterwards.[17] This example appears to encapsulate two points of view regarding the purpose of concealing horse skulls, those of foundation deposit and warding off evil.

The use of horse skulls as concealed deposits within buildings and in their foundations appears to be a very widespread tradition specifically to ward off evil. The idea that they were concealed for acoustic reasons seems to have developed from this original purpose, most likely as an excuse, and may have led to people experimenting with this as a form of acoustic enhancement.

However, the original use of the skulls to avert evil must have remained current during this period, for they continued to be used in ways that could not have produced acoustic benefit.

All this evidence leads to the inevitable question; why were horse skulls used, rather than any others? For this we need to look to the qualities of the horse in life. They are tame animals, useful to humans, and (in the British Isles) not a source of food. They can also be befriended, which is not something people generally do with livestock. They are highly sensitive creatures, capable of sensing things which humans cannot. Most importantly horses can sleep standing up with their eyes open – though they also sleep in the normal way, lying down with their eyes closed – and this gives them an appearance of vigilance through the night, when humans are sleeping.

The physical appearance of the horse skull is also important for their use as apotropaic object. When a horse skull is detached from the body, defleshed and cleaned, it is an impressive and fearsome-looking thing indeed. It seems likely that this, along with the horse's other qualities, were important factors in the use of their skulls. We could also consider many of the ancient legends of the horse, where they pull the chariot of the sun across the sky, or provide the method of travel between this world and the dead. The horse has occupied an important place in lore and folklore since prehistory.

Then there is the use of horseshoes as good luck charms throughout the British Isles, the USA, Europe and, it would seem, the rest of the world. In Britain and Ireland the preference is often to hang the horse shoes with points upwards, 'so that the luck doesn't run out'. In other parts of the world it's more usually pointing downwards. Obviously horseshoes are directly associated with the horse, and like the skulls should derive some of their power to avert evil just from this connection, but their frequent use at thresholds to buildings and the fact that they are made of iron are also important for their use as apotropaic objects. The fact that horses are shod with iron is significant in magical belief, as iron by itself wards off witchcraft.

The practice of concealing horse skulls in buildings must also be set against the widespread folk dances and traditions which also involve horses or horse skulls. The Hobby-Horse, the Mari Lwyd, soul-caking, the Hooden Horse and other folk customs were once very widespread with traditions in Wales, Kent, Lincolnshire, Cheshire and the south-west and in Ireland. Graffiti representing the Hobby-Horse can be found in a number of churches in Hertfordshire, a small testimony to their importance.

Although it is difficult to pin down a date of origin for these folk traditions, there are records of hobby-horses from as early as the fourteenth century.

They would often accompany folk dances and were sometimes also used in church collections. Hobby horses ranged in design from a pole draped in fabric and topped by a skull, to something smaller with model horse head at the end. The Mari Lwyd of south Wales – a man carrying a horse skull on a pole with a costume draped over it – first appears in records in the eighteenth century but may be considerably older; there was a similar tradition in Pembrokeshire.[18] When the Mari visits people's homes there is a preoccupation with sweeping, cleaning and in one song an association with the 'evil one' and the chimney.[19] These latter notes, however tenuous, suggest a link with sweeping away evil and protection of the hearth. There is something of a folk revival occurring at the present time with many people creating their own Maris and appearing at folk events.

These and other traditions attest to the impressive appearance of horse skulls, and an expectation that they would be in some way symbolic or powerful. We know that people were including horse skulls in new builds, particularly with chapels, at a time when these folk traditions and practices were still current, so it seems likely they had some awareness of the apotropaic functions of horse skulls in them too.

Before the advent and subsequent dominance of the motor vehicle as a form of transport, it was normal to encounter horses alive and well in everyday life. That was the visible, daytime experience of horses. Alongside this ran the folklore and magical beliefs around horses which is what gave them a parallel life beyond death which accidental discoveries and archaeological investigation are slowly revealing.

Notes
1. Brian Hoggard, 'Concealed animals', in *Physical Evidence for Ritual Acts, Sorcery and Witchcraft in Christian Britain: A Feeling for Magic*, ed. Ronald Hutton (Basingstoke: Palgrave Macmillan, 2016) pp.106–17; Brian Hoggard, *Magical House Protection: The Archaeology of Counter-Witchcraft* (New York: Berghahn, 2019) pp.55–63.
2. Albert Sandklef, *Singing Flails: A Study in Threshing-Floor Constructions, Flail Threshing Traditions and the Magic Guarding of the House*, FF Communications 56 (Helsinki: Academia Scientiarum Fennica, 1949).
3. Seán Ó Súilleabháin, 'Foundation sacrifices', *Journal of the Royal Society of Antiquaries of Ireland* 75 (1945) pp.49–50.
4. Ralph Merrifield, *The Archaeology of Ritual and Magic* (London: Batsford, 1987) p.123.
5. Philip Armitage, 'Gazetteer of sites with animal bones used as building material', in *Diet and Crafts in Towns: The Evidence of Animal Remains from*

the Roman to Post-Medieval Periods ed Dale Serjeantson and Tony Waldron, BAR British Series 199 (Oxford: BAR, 1989) pp.201–23.
6. Merrifield, *Archaeology of Ritual and Magic* p.118
7. Yvonne Hayhurst, 'A recent find of a horse skull in a house at Ballaugh, Isle of Man', *Folklore* 100 (1989) pp.105–7.
8. Nigel Pennick, 1986, *Skulls, Cats and Witch-bottles* (Privately published, 1986) p.6.
9. Rubyna Matthews, pers. comm.
10. Colm Moriarty 'Buried Horse Skulls: Folklore and Superstition in Early Modern Ireland' (2015): http://irisharchaeology.ie/2015/02/buried-horse-skulls-folklore-and-superstition-in-early-modern-ireland/, accessed February 2021.
11. Sonja Hukantaival, *'For a Witch Cannot Cross Such a Threshold!': Building Concealment Traditions in Finland c. 1200–1950*, Archaeologia Medii Aevi Finlandiae 23 (Turku: Suomen Keskiajan Arkeologian Seura, 2016); and cf. Sonja Hukantaival, 'Horse skulls and alder-horse: the horse as a depositional sacrifice in buildings', in *The Horse and Man in European Antiquity: Worldview, Burial Rites and Military and Everyday Life*, ed Audronė Bliujienė (Klaipėda : Klaipėda University Press, 2009) pp.350–6.
12. Eurwyn Wiliam, 'Concealed horse skulls – testimony and message' in *From Corrib to Cultra: Folklife Essays in Honour of Alan Gailey* ed Trefor Owen (Belfast: Queen's University Belfast, 2000) pp.136–49.
13. Enid Porter, *Cambridgeshire Customs and Folklore* (Chatham: Routledge, 1969) p.181.
14. John Donaldson, *An Historical and Statistical Account of the Barony of Upper Fews in the County of Armagh in 1838* (Dundalk: Dundalgan Press, 1923) p.77.
15. Wiliam, 'Concealed horse skulls' p.138.
16. Rocky and Kathy Foley 'Bryant's surprise', *Old House Journal* 19 (1991) pp.49–50.
17. Ellis Bryn, *Halkyn Mountain Communities in Times Past* (Privately published, 1993) p.40.
18. Edwin Christopher Cawte, *Ritual Animal Disguise* (Ipswich: Folklore Society, 1978) pp.10–47.
19. Cawte, Ritual Animal Disguise pp.99–101.

Rethinking the Perception of Magic and Rituals in Archaeological Contexts and in Material Culture: A three-fold dialogue between field archaeologists, academics, and the public

Debora Moretti

Introduction

In December 2012, the 34th annual conference of the Theoretical Archaeology Group, held at the University of Liverpool, hosted a very special session organised by Ceri Houlbrook and Natalie Armitage, at the time PhD candidates at the University of Manchester. The session, which they had titled 'The Materiality of Magic: An Artefactual Investigation into Ritual Practices and Popular Beliefs', resulted from their belief that 'magic, materially manifested, deserves academic attention, and that the archaeological perspective is particularly applicable to its study'.[1]

The session proved to be so popular that the lecture room originally booked for it had to be changed for a larger one. It was very successful and the papers were gathered in an edited volume published in 2015.[2] Covering a wide chronological and geographical span, these addressed the neglect of magic in academic circles and provided cross-cultural case studies showing how material manifestations of magic can help us understand past and present cultures. As importantly, they highlight the methodological issues and difficulties which we face when we try to interpret structured deposits, ritual middens, and ritual deposits made by people before or without writing in a context where we cannot cross-reference across disciplines to records of folklore or written texts.

This TAG session followed up a complex and challenging debate, some thirty years old at the time, which had looked for evidence of magic and witchcraft practices in archaeological contexts and in broader evidence of material culture.

It is in connection with this materiality of magic that archaeology has become more and more important in the study of ancient magic and witchcraft; it has also increasingly come to support history when we seek a better understanding of how magic and witchcraft beliefs have developed and evolved from antiquity to modern times.[3]

One of the starting points of this debate lay in the development of cognitive archaeology. Cognitive archaeology is a *physical* approach since it engages with the human past through the evidence of material remains, but it is also a *cognitive* approach because it studies past ways of thought as inferred from that evidence – a definition made by Colin Renfrew in his seminal work *The Making of the Human Mind*.[4]

In the early 1980s, prominent archaeologists were worried by the lack of interest shown by contemporary archaeological theories – above all processual archaeology – when they came to the thoughts and beliefs of ancient people. Discussing the division between mind and matter in archaeology in *Towards an Archaeology of the Mind* (1982), Renfrew stated:

> The gap cannot be bridged, nor can 'mind' usefully be considered when taken in isolation from its 'thoughts'. These thoughts, I assert, or some of them do find effective expression in the material record.[5]

At that moment the seed of the 'archaeology of the mind' was planted in the fertile soil of theoretical archaeology, and cognitive archaeology was the next logical step. Meanings and symbols became important, and factors of 'human agency' introduced to what had been a mechanical and functional analysis of material evidence.

From this point forward the archaeology of the mind developed and it narrowed its goal. Cognitive archaeology differed from hermeneutic or interpretative archaeology – which focused on the recovery of the meanings of the objects that had been found – by its focus on 'how the minds of the ancient communities... worked, and the manner in which that working, shaped their actions', and how these actions were reflected in the material evidence.[6]

Unless they have been written down, preserved and transmitted in literary form, the belief systems and thought processes of past societies can only be inferred from an extremely careful investigation and interpretation of the material culture of a specific society or group, and the behavioural processes that created this material culture. It was the theory of cognitive evolution and the interpretation of this evolution using archaeological data that lay behind the development of cognitive archaeology.[7]

More specifically, cognitive archaeology:

> deals with concepts and perceptions... the whole spectrum of human behaviour, with especial reference to religion and beliefs, symbolism and iconography, and the development and expression of human consciousness based on the surviving material evidence. Probably the most exhaustive categories studied by cognitive archaeology are

cosmology, religion, ideology and iconography.[8]

There are many approaches and studies existing under the umbrella term 'cognitive archaeology' but they can be grouped under three main branches. These are post-processual archaeology, cognitive-processual archaeology and evolutionary-cognitive archaeology.

Of these three, the cognitive-processual school – which focuses on how specific symbols are used in specific contexts – is perhaps methodologically the most appropriate for studying beliefs in magic and witchcraft. When Renfrew explains the connection between cognition and symbols through six main categories, the fifth consists of symbols used 'in coping with the supernatural, by mediating between the human and the world beyond'.[9]

The academic debate on cognitive science in the study of magic and witchcraft remains extremely lively, as represented in the controversial but innovative work of Edward Bever on *Realities of Witchcraft and Popular Magic in Early Modern Europe: Culture, Cognition and Everyday Life*, and the subsequent debate in a forum section of the journal *Magic, Ritual and Witchcraft* and other specialised periodicals.[10]

In archaeology the cognitive approach has been applied to studies of magic and witchcraft swiftly – but not without methodological issues – since the late 1980s, at a time when interest in the materiality of magic and witchcraft developed generally as part of a wider recent trend in the study of material culture.[11]

Beliefs and practices connected to magic and witchcraft were not only witnessed by words and actions. They were also represented by texts, amulets, curse tablets and many other objects which have left material evidence which, when analysed and studied correctly, can give us important clues to magic and witchcraft beliefs.[12]

Among many scholars, the one who stands out for the first and most complete contribution to the archaeological study of magic and witchcraft in Britain is of course Ralph Merrifield. In 1987 Merrifield published *The Archaeology of Ritual and Magic*, a survey of material objects indicating the existence of ritualistic and magical behaviour.[13] These came from different contexts – Roman and early Anglo-Saxon but also medieval and early modern. For the first time continuity in ritual deposits was demonstrated from pagan and Christian contexts alike, which – if not indicating or even implying a continuity in the same beliefs – showed that certain ritual practices shared a similar modality throughout time.[14]

The main point of Merrifield's work is perfectly explained in his own words:

> All who have any interest in that wide field of human thought, aspiration, and fears, covered by such terms as 'religion', 'magic', and the more derogatory 'superstition', will be fully aware that it has produced immense activity that must have left almost as many traces in the archaeological record as any of the basic human activities that are concerned with satisfying hunger, constructing shelter, or providing defence against enemies.

Furthermore, his work brought attention to two major issues: the stubborn reluctance of medieval and early modern archaeologists and historians – hidden behind methodological and interpretative 'defensive barricades' – to engage with material evidence for magic and ritual; and a general lack of understanding and misinterpretating of archaeological deposits which suggested magical activity.[15]

Since then, the study of magic and witchcraft in archaeological contexts has developed further by implementing the cognitive-processual approach, but the two major methodological issues identified by Merrifield remain. They were to be addressed by different academics throughout the years.

Brian Hoggard, for example, began an article on 'The archaeology of folk magic' in 1999 by saying: 'In this article I hope to draw the readers' attention to a little-known field of study known as the archaeology of folk magic'.[16] This highlighted how little archaeologists and historians knew or understood the study of magic and witchcraft. In the same year he started a survey of objects related to magic and witchcraft practices in Britain, during which 661 museums, innumerable archaeological units and private individuals were contacted and provided the materials.[17]

The old limitations persisted, to be further addressed by Roberta Gilchrist in her 2012 book *Medieval Life*, with a chapter addressing the connections between people and buildings and the placement of 'special deposits' within buildings.[18] In a previous article 'Magic for the dead? The archaeology of magic in later medieval burials' she pin-points the core issue:

> It may be that archaeologists studying the Middle Ages have found the juxtaposition of magic and Christianity difficult to interrogate, based on the false assumption that these are mutually exclusive categories comprising marginal superstition on the one hand versus formalised religion on the other.[19]

The 2012 TAG session attempted to address these issues. More recently, the issue has been addressed by *Physical Evidence for Ritual Acts: Sorcery and Witchcraft in Christian Britain*, edited by Ronald Hutton in 2016, which confirms the long reluctance of archaeologists and historians to approach material evidence of magic in Christian contexts but also demonstrates a general, gradual but welcome change of attitude towards this topic. The archaeology of magic rides on the back of a wider historical interest in the magic and witchcraft of medieval and early modern Europe.[20]

Physical Evidence offers more than an updated bibliography of studies on the material evidence of magic and witchcraft; it is itself part of this new wave of research, studying objects and architectural markings 'revealed by casual discovery or collected from owners' which showed continuity in magic ritual practices from medieval to modern Christian Britain.

The Core of the Issue

For me, as one of the speakers, that 2012 TAG session represented a pivotal moment. My archaeological background is in Italy, where thanks to the Etruscan and Roman civilisations, magic practices have been imbedded in the world-view over different cultural periods, and magic practices are blatantly obvious in the archaeological record. So the very British resistance to everything that is ritual was new to me. And this amplified my interest on the topic.

From the very beginning of my archaeological career, I have focussed on understanding the physical evidence for rituals and magic in archaeological contexts. Early in my studies I fell in love with the idea that the beliefs and practices connected with magic and witchcraft were represented, not only by words and actions, but also by objects. Material culture leaves evidence which, when analysed and studied correctly, offers clues not just to magical thinking but to the wider belief systems of the past. And yet I felt how limiting it was for the one discipline of archaeology to be called on to deal with such a ubiquitous topic.

Magic and witchcraft are extremely hard to categorise. Their perception changes from culture to culture, from place to place, and of course from one historic period to another. To overcome the limitations of a purely archaeological approach I expanded my horizons, studying magic from an historical and ethnographical viewpoint. For this, I undertook a PhD program at the University of Bristol, part of the project 'The Figure of the Witch' funded by the Leverhulme Trust and led by Professor Ronald Hutton. My thesis examined the perception of image of the witch and witchcraft in medieval and early modern Italy, drawing on the archive of the Roman Inquisition and ethnographical sources from the Archive of the Folk Traditions of Maremma (in Tuscany), together with archaeo-linguistic data.

To better understand perceptions of magic and witchcraft through time, I became a multi-disciplinary researcher, an inbetweener with a micro-approach to a macro-phenomenon which showed me the limitations of a purely archaeological approach to magic and witchcraft. In doing so I looked for ways to bridge the obvious gaps in the archaeological approach and to overcome its limitations in dealing with evidence for magic and witchcraft practices in archaeological contexts.

The most notable gap between the different disciplines was their uneven interest in the material culture of magic and witchcraft. Whereas history, folklore and anthropology have expanded and intensified the study of magic and witchcraft in the last two decades, archaeology has fallen behind since Merrifield's book was published. Surprisingly, it was specifically field archaeology which had lost its way.

Magic is perennially fascinating to the wider public. Recently this fascination has taken hold of academia, and advances in the study of magical practices from antiquity to modern Europe have created historical narratives which engage, entice, and inspire future academics as well as the general public. One obvious example was the incredible success of the exhibition *Spellbound* at the Ashmolean Museum in late 2018. The international conference kick-starting this exhibition sparked a lively discussion between historians and archaeologists on methodological approaches and the lack of multidisciplinary dialogues on the study of material evidence connected to magic and witchcraft.

Despite the increased interest at theoretical and academic level in physical evidence of magic and witchcraft beliefs, conference attenders felt that at practical level – during the actual archaeological excavations or incidental discoveries of these objects – neglect and misinterpretation are still standard. This problem could perhaps be rectified in research-led archaeology by introducing students to the topic, either in advance during their university courses, or by target-training during excavations; but this cannot be done in developer-led archaeology.

Not everybody realises that 90% of the archaeological investigations currently undertaken in Britain are carried out by commercial archaeological organisations and in projects initiated by development.[21] Four-fifths of the archaeological data collected in Britain comes from developer-led excavations which, unlike research archaeology, are carried out to offset the impact that development has on the historic environment and are therefore financed directly by the developers. This has a heavy impact on the timescale of every project and the budget available for post-excavation analysis.

Developer-led archaeologists work on a tight budget and keep to tight schedules. In most cases, therefore, it is impossible to convince them – and I should know, as I have been a commercial archaeologist since 2006 – that a rolled-up piece of lead in an ancient ditch or post-hole is not just a random piece of lead thrown away but the physical evidence of magic activity; and it is as impossible to persuade contractors working on a building that a shoe in a chimney is not just a random shoe somehow lost up there but the symbol of an apotropaic act.

Considering how much archaeological data comes into academic research from development-based excavations, it is worrying to find such huge gaps in knowledge and data-processing when it comes to apotropaic material culture and magical traditions.

So, after the heated debate at the Spellbound conference in September 2019, I decided to investigate the apparent lack of interest of field archaeologists on magic/witchcraft evidence in archaeological contexts, and to find reasons for the apparent lack of knowledge of the topic. I therefore carried out a little survey of my colleagues working in commercial archaeology, asking standard questions to probe their assumed lack of interest:
1) Do you think medieval/early modern apotropaic/magic material culture is worth recording?
2) Would you be able to identify – in the field – any of the objects belonging to the main categories of what we consider medieval and early modern apotropaic/magic material culture?
3) What impact would the inclusion of apotropaic/magic material evidence in the routine of commercial archaeology methodology have on time schedules and budgets?

The responses followed a standard pattern. Everybody that I spoke to agreed on the fascination and interest of the topic. Everybody agreed that apotropaic material culture is worth recording but – this is the main point – confessed they would be unable to identify objects indicating possible magical traditions, and that in any case it would not be feasible to look for them in development-funded excavations following the methodologies currently implemented in commercial archaeology.

These responses present a very logical and financially focused *modus operandi* which, as an archaeological project manager of a commercial company, I understand and appreciate. We must be competitive and at the same time able to follow guidelines and methodologies to the letter in order to preserve the archaeological record; we must be able to please clients, consultants, local authorities, and the public; we must do all that while digging in all weather conditions as fast and as accurately as we can, knowing that we must do our job to the best of our ability because the principle of commercial archaeology is preservation by record. This means that once we have excavated, interpreted, and recorded an archaeological feature, this will be destroyed and will only survive in records. Our record!

The apparent lack of interest or knowledge in the topic is therefore not a reflection of individual field archaeologists; it is something endemic to the profession itself, a consequence of our reliance on well-known and regularly updated guidelines and methodologies created by the specific governing bodies.[22]

CIfA (the Chartered Institute for Archaeologists) is, with Historic England, the main governing body for professional archaeologists. In 2019, following my survey, I addressed the annual conference of CIfA with a paper recommending that the Institute take a closer look at this issue and develop an official methodology and strategy which would support and educate field archaeologists in commercial archaeology to make space for apotropaic and magic material culture. I stressed that we should all remember that professional field archaeologists are not just diggers. We are all, especially with the rapid disappearance of archaeological studies from academia, the keepers of our heritage; we are literally the physical barrier between our heritage and the machines of demolition; and as such we should be given the credit and the support to be able to perform our role within our own job specification and inspire the wider public with their own cultural and historical heritage, represented in this case by objects indicating a past spiritual belief system. There should be guidelines in place to allow the identification of the signs that such beliefs might be possible, and there should be time to critically interpret them before they disappear forever in the bucket of an excavator.

My paper was well received by the audience, consisting mainly of field archaeologists, but CIfA granted me no feedback at all despite my later request to create workshops specifically designed to cover the topic and set up a specialist group to provide support to field archaeologists.

For this reason, I decided to make the wider public aware of this issue, as I feel that until the study of the material evidence of magic and witchcraft reaches mainstream archaeological literature, and we change our modern attitude to magical traditions of the past, a good percentage of this material evidence will end up in boxes on the shelves of archaeological units' warehouses or in spoil heaps and skips.

Conclusions

Many recent trends have helped promote study of the physical evidence for magic and witchcraft, amongst them the wider interest in material culture and the advances made in historical witchcraft studies; but despite this momentum, the status of this study within the archaeological discipline still suffers from all the methodological issues originally identified by Ralph Merrifield in 1987. Although being fully embraced by academic or research-led archaeology – as demonstrated by Brian Hoggard's recent book *Magical House Protection: The Archaeology of Counter-Witchcraft*, and the latest work by Owen Davies and Ceri Houlbrook, *Building Magic: Ritual and Re-Enchantment in Post-Medieval Structures*– the topic is still almost absent from field archaeology.[23] Almost but not quite, since Owen Davies and Ceri Houlbrook have collaborated with Nigel Jeffries from Mola on the project 'Bottles Concealed and Revealed: Examining the Phenomena of Stone and Glass 'Witch Bottles' and their Concealment in Mid to Late 17th-Century England'.

Despite all this, Merrifield's statement on the 'general lack of understanding and the misinterpretation of deposits indicating magical activity in archaeological contexts' still applies where it matters most: in the field. This needs to be rectified with the creation and implementation of specific guidelines by the governing bodies, with inclusion of this topic in Historic and Environment Records regional research agendas and most of all, with the creation of learning tools for field archaeologists and post-excavation officers. Because ultimately if we, field/professional archaeologists, are no longer inspired to understand important aspects of our own past and culture, and if this understanding is not fully supported by our governing bodies, then how can we leave an accurate record of the archaeological sites disappearing with development, and how can we inspire the wider public and future generations?

Notes

1. Ceri Houlbrook and Natalie Armitage, 'Introduction' in *The Materiality of Magic: An Artefactual Investigation into Ritual Practices and Popular Beliefs* ed Ceri Houlbrook and Natalie Armitage (Oxford: Oxbow, 2015) pp.1–13 at p.1.
2. Houlbrook and Armitage, eds., *Materiality of Magic*.
3. Debora Moretti, 'The Witch and the Shaman: Elements of Paganism and

Regional Differences in Italian Witches' Trials', unpublished PhD Thesis, University of Bristol (2018) p.63.
4. Colin Renfrew, *Prehistory: The Making of the Human Mind* (London: Phoenix, 2007) p.107.
5. Colin Renfrew, *Towards an Archaeology of the Mind* (Cambridge: Cambridge University Press, 1982) p.27.
6. Moretti, 'The Witch and the Shaman' p.64.
7. For the theory of cognitive evolution see Merlin Donald, *Origins of the Modern Mind* (Cambridge, MA: Harvard University Press, 1991); Colin Renfrew and Chris Scarre, *Cognition and Material Culture : The Archaeology of Symbolic Storage* (Cambridge: Cambridge University Press 1998); Renfrew, *Prehistory*. For cognitive archaeology in general see Colin Renfrew, *Towards an Archaeology of the Mind* (Cambridge: Cambridge University Press, 1982); Colin Renfrew and Ezra Zubrow, eds., *The Ancient Mind: Elements of Cognitive Archaeology* (Cambridge: Cambridge University Press, 1993).
8. Colin Renfrew et al., 'What is cognitive archaeology ?', *Cambridge Archaeological Journal*, 3 (1993) pp.247-70 at p.247.
9. Renfrew et al., 'What is cognitive archaeology?' p.249.
10. Edward Bever, *Realities of Witchcraft and Popular Magic in Early Modern Europe: Culture, Cognition and Everyday Life* (London, New York: Palgrave Macmillan, 2008); Edward Bever, 'Current trends in the application of cognitive science to magic', *Magic, Ritual, and Witchcraft* 7 (2012) pp.3-18; Stuart Clark, 'One-tier history', *Magic, Ritual and Witchcraft* 5 (2010) pp.84-90; Richard Jenkins, 'Reality, but not as we know it', *Magic, Ritual, and Witchcraft* 5 (2010) pp.91-5; Rita Voltmer, 'Behind the "veil of memory": about the limitations of narrative', *Magic, Ritual, and Witchcraft* 5 (2010) pp.96-102; Willem De Blécourt, 'Witchcraft – discourse and disappearance: Württemberg and the Dutch documentation', *Magic, Ritual, and Witchcraft* 5 (2010) pp.103-7; Jesper Sørensen, 'Magic as a state of mind? Neurocognitive theory and magic in early modern Europe', *Magic, Ritual, and Witchcraft* 5 (2010) pp.108-12; Edward Bever, 'The critiques and The Realities', *Magic, Ritual, and Witchcraft* 5 (2010) pp.113-21.
11. Dan Hicks, 'The material-cultural turn: event and effect', in *The Oxford Handbook of Material Culture Studies* ed. D. Hicks and M.C. Beaudry (Oxford: Oxford University Press, 2010) pp.25-99; Harvey Green, 'Cultural history and the material(s) turn', *Cultural History* 1 (2012) pp.61-82.
12. Debora Moretti, 'Binding spells and curse tablets through time', in *The Materiality of Magic* ed. Houlbrook & Armitage pp.103-22.
13. Ralph Merrifield, *The Archaeology of Ritual and Magic* (London: Batsford, 1987).

14. Merrifield, *Archaeology of Ritual and Magic* p.115.
15. Merrifield, *Archaeology of Ritual and Magic* pp.83–106, 184–94.
16. Brian Hoggard, 'The archaeology of folk magic', *White Dragon* 23 (1999) pp.17–20 at p.17.
17. Brian Hoggard, 'The archaeology of counter-witchcraft and popular magic', in *Beyond the Witch Trials: Witchcraft and Magic in Enlightenment Europe* ed. Owen Davis and Willem De Blécourt (Manchester: Manchester University Press, 2004) pp.167–86 at p.169; www.apotropaios.co.uk (accessed December 2021).
18. Roberta Gilchrist, *Medieval Life: Archaeology and the Life Course* (Woodbridge: Boydell Press, 2012) pp.216–52.
19. Roberta Gilchrist, 'Magic for the dead? The archaeology of magic in later medieval burials', *Medieval Archaeology* 52 (2008) pp.119–59 at p.120.
20. Ronald Hutton, ed., *Physical Evidence for Ritual Acts, Sorcery and Witchcraft in Christian Britain: A Feeling for Magic* (Basingstoke: Palgrave Macmillan, 2016).
21. John Curtis *et al.*, *History for the Taking? Perspectives on Material Heritage* (London: The British Academy, 2011) p.33.
22. https://www.archaeologists.net/codes/cifa; https://historicengland.org.uk/advice/find/latest-guidance/ (both accessed December 2021).
23. Brian Hoggard, *Magical House Protection: The Archaeology of Counter-Witchcraft* (New York: Berghahn, 2019); Owen Davies and Ceri Houlbrook, *Building Magic: Ritual and Re-enchantment in Post-Medieval Structures* (Basingstoke: Palgrave Macmillan 2021).

Arrow Sharpening Marks: An English church myth

Jeremy Harte

The traveller who visits St. Michael's Shotwick will be surprised to see that, in the otherwise well-maintained porch of a Cheshire church, the masonry above the benches has been scored deeply in parallel grooves. There are about twenty of these on a wall, one after another, running over three blocks of stone. There is no missing them and naturally you wonder what they are, but not for long, because the guide has a story to enlighten you.

> Our church porch bears witness to another activity carried on near the church. By a decree of Edward III, after Mass the rest of Sunday had to be devoted to the sport of archery, all other sport being prohibited in its interest. The grooves worn in the stones in the porch were made by archers sharpening their arrows before practice at the butts. No wonder these deadly English archers won Agincourt, Crecy and Poitiers against armoured troops, as the English 6ft bow when drawn fully to the right ear could drive an arrow through an oak door 4 inches thick. The fields to the west of the church were still called 'The Butts' on the 1843 tithe map.[1]

Well, here is two for one: not just a set of ancient marks in the church fabric, but a story to go with them. It's not quite a legend, for it does not contain anything which would stretch our credulity, like a witch or a dragon or a mound where the fairies play: but it tells us of heroic deeds in days gone by, and the clinching evidence consists of marks on old stone and a place-name, which is exactly how you round off the narrative in legends of a more supernatural kind.

And, like a legend, this story is told at place after place, each one proudly putting forward the common narrative as a special tradition of their own church. Studying the facts about Shotwick and other sites is therefore a double project: in order to trace the story of the stories – how they first came to be told, and why – you have to evaluate what the grooves really are and how they came to be made. I shall call them arrow sharpening marks, although as we shall see they may not strictly have been marks, were useless for sharpening, and have nothing to do with arrows. It would be unEnglish to let tradition be faced down by logic, and besides, the phrase is already widely current online.

Yardley in Warwickshire is now more or less a suburb of Birmingham, which is as central within England as you can get, and here St. Edburgha's has its own set of marks, cut near the base of the tower and in the course of masonry just above it, looking exactly like the Cheshire ones at Shotwick.[2] Go down to the South-West and you will find them on red Devon sandstone in a buttress of the church at Totnes; go up to the North Riding and you will find them in the church of the porch at Thirsk.[3] Wherever they are found, arrow sharpening marks are made in a uniform style. They are vertical slots, sometimes parallel-sided, sometimes in the shape of a slender boat's keel, varying slightly in depth as if each mark had been made by repeated scraping until the groove was about half an inch deep, at which point it became inconvenient to work it further and a new one was started. Although each mark must have begun as a narrow line, they are spaced out so they do not overlap when widened. They are set low in the building, sometimes very low indeed.

Fig. 1. Thirsk church, North Riding of Yorkshire.

They can be found in parallel strings on a single course of masonry, or on two, one above the other. Aston upon Trent in Derbyshire stands at the limit with marked blocks on four successive courses, and even that may be the work of repair masons resetting the stones.[4] Where there are marks on a stone, they will cover that stone before they move onto the next one, and they stick within the boundaries of the block, which means that they do not normally run to more than six or eight inches high. This is because they are normally cut into horizontal walling stones, although at Ashprington in Devon and Broughton in Lincolnshire the marks are longer because they extend almost all the height of a vertical shaft.[5]

There is danger here for the over-classifying mind, as there is with all archaeological categories. Have we picked on a type-site like Shotwick, and treated everything that resembles it as a 'proper' arrow sharpening mark, disregarding the ones that don't fit? There are certainly some outliers. Typically, marks are vertical; I doubt whether there are any horizontal ones, although it is easy to mistake eroded fault lines in base-bedded sandstone for deliberate marks. But in conversation at the Chester conference some people reported seeing diagonal marks. Again, they are typically in sandstone or other sedimentary rocks, but examples have been found on limestone blocks.

Geological variations in building stone would explain the limited distribution of arrow sharpening marks. The counties from which they have been most often reported are Devon, Worcestershire, Warwickshire, Shropshire, Staffordshire and Derbyshire – typically on red sandstones or millstone grit, in other words on good building stone which can nevertheless be scraped without too much difficulty to form a groove. Where a church wall contains stone from more than one quarry, it is always the softest blocks which are selected for marks, though these would have been the least useful as whetstones. So far as I know, marks are absent from churches on the great building belt of fine oolite limestone which runs diagonally across England from Lyme to Lincoln, and they seldom appear south and east of this line.

Fig. 2. Checkley church, Staffordshire.

Marks of the classic kind are also found in Scotland – on the Borders, in Fife, and up as far as Dunlichty in Inverness-shire. There are some variations which suggest that we may be outside the heartland of the tradition: for instance, the grooves at Stobo Kirk in Peebles are shallow lines scored continuously over three courses of masonry, not confined to one block at a time as in the English Midlands.[6] But what look like regional variations may simply reflect the way in which different building stones respond to being scored with a metal point.

This assumes that we know how the marks were made. They must have been created by metal, because nothing else would cut grooves in stone, but the tradition that they were created by sharpening arrows will not stand up to practical scrutiny. This point has already been made by James Wright, online and in a forthcoming publication; already by the time of the conference, it was clear that we had been thinking about this problem on parallel lines, and in what follows I am doing little more than recapitulating his argument.[7]

Fig. 3. Stobo kirk, Peebles-shire.

Firstly, archers sharpen their arrows just as you would, if you were putting an edge on a pen-knife or any other short tool: by drawing the blade sideways on a sharpening stone, or by filing a whetstone against it. Running an arrowhead in a groove would simply make it blunt, while rubbing it up and down would be virtually impossible. Since arrowheads were already mounted onto a shaft – those from the Mary Rose were 31½ inches long – it would be awkward to manipulate them against a fixed stone and common sense suggests the use of files and whetstones.[8]

Secondly, medieval archers did not always carry quivers; it was just as common for arrows to be tucked down into a belt, with the heads facing frontwards. This isn't something that modern re-enactors could get away with in their risk assessments, especially for hunting arrows, the type which needed the keenest edge. It is easy to see how one stumble in the woods could send the arrow slicing forward and down through a femoral artery. Self-preservation required that they should be left as blunt as possible until arrival at the hunting station.

Thirdly, the arrows used in archery practice were not sharp at all. Target shooting was done with piles, arrows ending in a rounded head; some of these taper like a bullet, others are domed at the tip. The archers at practice in the Luttrell Psalter are shooting arrows with little stubby heads.[9] This again was common sense: practice is about shooting into the target, not through it, and sharp arrows would only have increased the danger for bystanders.

Ready-sharpened arrows would only have been of use in times of war – although war-bows with a draw weight of over 100lb could, you imagine, have shot anything through anything. In the Hundred Years War the use of barbed bodkins, which were solid-pointed with slight wings on either side, represented a compromise between the penetrating head and the flesh-cutting barbs.[10] But like hunting arrows these must have been sharpened on site, with whetstones. The embrasures built for defensive archery in fortifications, which are the one place we know to have been staffed by bored bowmen who needed to make their arrows keen, never contain arrow sharpening marks. In fact whenever the marks are found in towns which actually had fortifications, like Totnes and Weddington Castle, the marks are on the church – the one place where arrows were not needed.[11]

In short, the association of these marks with real arrows and bowmen is quite impossible: it is just another of the stories that Jennifer Westwood used to call old men's fancies, superficially plausible antiquarian guesswork which has been repeated from guide to guide, not because there was any evidence for it, but because something about it gripped the imagination, and because anything can pass for true when it has already been told about somewhere else. The very definition of folklore, in fact. Of course it would clinch the counter-argument if we could point to arrow sharpening marks and say why they were *really* made. But that is not so easy.

The typical place for marks, as at Shotwick, is in the church porch: more than half are found there, on all parts of the structure. Some are on the outside wall, as at Totnes and Kenton in Devon. At Stokeingteignhead in Devon, Shrawley in Worcestershire, Thorpe in Derbyshire and Great Urswick in Lancashire they appear on the external archway, sometimes facing outwards to the church path, sometimes cut on the line of the arch. Offchurch in Warwickshire has them inside the porch, as do Lambley in Nottinghamshire and Shotwick. At Ashprington in Devon and Whetstone in Leicestershire the marks are cut in the arch of the door leading into the church.[12]

At Mugginton in Derbyshire, the thirteenth-century church door has no porch. Capitals on either side testify to flanking shafts, now gone; on the left the space behind is deeply cut away by marks, which extend outwards onto the wall. Here a block in the upper course has been so reduced by marks that it looks more like folded drapery than stone, although curiously the masonry to the right of the door is untouched.[13] At Appleton Wiske in Yorkshire a much simpler doorway has four arrow marks on a single block of stone to the right – significantly, the one soft sandstone block in the arch. The door has now been blocked, evidently after the marks were made.[14]

Fig. 4. Naunton Beauchamp church, Worcestershire.

Marks are also found away from doorways, usually in walls to the left of the porch. At Burton Hastings in Warwickshire they are on the base of the tower, just above the foundation plinth and below the batter course, the one which protrudes in a slope to throw rainwater away from the footings. At Middleton in the same county they are above the batter course; at Yardley above and on this course. Naunton Beauchamp in Worcestershire has a long series of marks just under the batter course. Here as on other heavily scored blocks such as Thirsk, Middleton, Kenton and Thorpe, the work of cutting grooves has been carried on with such gusto that the whole block is dished. It is noticeable that all these marks on towers are cut low down, within three or four feet of the ground.

Slightly higher are those made on the window sill at Stoke Golding in

Leicestershire. Here again the window is to the left of the porch and marks stretch along the two courses of the sill and the batter course underneath it. There are other marks on a window ledge at Weddington Castle in Warwickshire.

Buttresses, usually near the porch, have been selected for marks at Checkley in Staffordshire, Packwood in Warwickshire, and Paignton in Devon.

This is all impressionistic, based on searches for the recurrent arrow sharpening story rather than systematic observation, but it has thrown up patterns which could be confirmed by more regular fieldwork. Marks are confined to small areas, at or below waist height; they cluster around the entrance, or are found on the walls to its left. I think we are dealing with 'entrance' and 'left' here, not liturgical 'south' and 'west'; although most porches are on the south side of the church, marks are found in the regular way on the north porch at Stokeinteignhead. What mattered was that they should be near the way in. At least one site, Alveley in Shropshire, has marks on the coping stones of the churchyard wall, on either side of the lychgate.[15] A proper survey, of the kind undertaken for medieval graffiti, might find more.

Fig. 5. Stoke Golding church, Leicestershire.

A few churches have internal marks, although these tend to depart from the regular pattern. Grooves on a pillar of the nave at Dunton Bassett in Leicestershire include one wide boat-shaped cut made on the edge, not the face, of the pillar; it is in a comparatively resistant limestone, and has other slighter grooves inside it.[16] At Wilford in Nottinghamshire there are marks on the chancel walls, although as these have been thought to date from a time when the chancel was unused and open to the sky, they may count as external.[17] At Broughton in Lincolnshire a single sandstone block in the northern angle-shaft of the chancel arch has been worn away by repeated grooves – seven or eight are still visible, running the whole height of the block, but they must have been the last of many as the block is almost completely worn away.[18]

A similar location on the tower arch is deeply scored with marks in the church at Berwick in Sussex. Like other internal marks, these are atypical; instead of a few deep grooves set in parallel, there are more than forty shallow ones crowded into two blocks of stone, some overlapping, and carrying on unbroken into the courses above and below.[19] Maybe people who were actually in the church did not have the time or opportunity to make deeper incisions. There are a few marks like this on monumental effigies. John Billingsley found dozens on a medieval tomb at Beetham in Westmorland, and I have seen scored lines which could be interpreted this way on a fourteenth-century tomb recess, now set in the external wall at Clun in Shropshire.

Of course the dates of these monuments only provide a *terminus a quo*; since most stonework in a church is medieval, it is tempting to assume that marks on it must be nearly as old, but we don't know how long the tombs, pillars, or arches had stood before people began scoring lines on them. At Suckley in Worcestershire, the socket stone of a cross in the churchyard is deeply cut on all four sides with marks which slant inwards to the space where the shaft once stood; they must have been made after the Reformation, when the cross itself was taken away.[20] Arrow sharpening marks are also found on secular buildings. In Scotland there are examples on the castles of Doune and Dirleton, and on that of Stirling, which is known to have been built between 1540 and 1542.[21] At Felsted sacred and secular were closely combined in Tudor times when the guildhall adjoining the church became a school, and graffiti can be found on the wooden archway through the old building, the timbers of its back wall, and the adjoining Riche Chapel, which was completed by 1617. Among the graffiti are several deep grooves, carved in sets of three, which must therefore be seventeenth-century.[22] Marks are found on the church porch of Barton-in-Fabis in Nottinghamshire, which was built at the end of the seventeenth century.[23]

Fig. 6. Suckley churchyard, preaching cross, Worcestershire.

Fig. 7. Solihull church, Warwickshire.

At Solihull in Warwickshire they appear on the church wall to the left of a doorway of 1535, and may be later than that, since the arrow sharpening marks are mixed with and respect circular cup marks which look very much as if they were made by turning a coin round and round.[24] Cheap copper currency wasn't available until the late seventeenth century so if this was being used the cups, and the accompanying grooves, must be later than that. At Mayfield in Sussex, marks appear in the usual way on three or four blocks of the south wall of the church, but one block is a defective repair which has been chocked up on a fill of mortar and brick. This block has marks which fit within its irregular outline and must therefore be later than the modern brick fill. Perhaps if we were less focussed on the Middle Ages, we might find similar marks on brickwork or other post-medieval structures. One set has been reported from a gravestone of 1706 at Kenilworth.[25]

So what are these marks? The arrow sharpening explanation has driven most others out of the field – although at Stobo Kirk, John Buchan was told children made the marks sharpening their slate pencils to be ready for school, in the days when this was held inside the church. Wilfrid Bonser visited Yardley in the 1950s, where he was told about arrow sharpening but took it sceptically.[26] Instead he preferred the theory put forward by Charles Leland in 1897, who thought that marks were made ritually by women who wanted children. He had seen this being done in Egypt, where young wives knelt around the walls of an old temple and scraped a groove with a knife or a sharp stone as a charm to get pregnant.[27] There may be something to this

Fig. 8. Yardley church, Warwickshire.

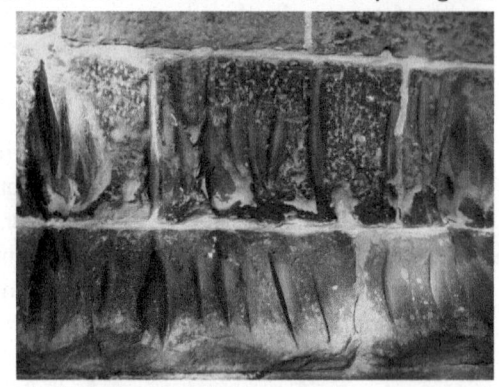

– many of our marks, such as those at Naunton Beauchamp, were clearly made by someone on their knees – but the Egyptian custom was a private ritual at a secret place, whereas the south front of a village church is about as public as you can get.

Could marks have been associated with formal religion rather than superstition? The one on the pillar in Dunton Bassett church is so wide, and so conspicuous on the corner of the stonework, that it looks like the Wound of Christ, a popular subject for late medieval devotion. At Kenton in Devon the marks are under a stoup to the left of the porch – not on the hard stone of the stoup itself but on softer blocks nearby. Marks at Crail in Fife were made by the window just under a consecration cross. But there is no coherent pattern of associations here, and the juxtapositions may just be coincidence.

At Yardley they now have another explanation for the marks. Marriage guests wanted to throw something over the bride and groom, as the posh people did at weddings: they didn't have confetti, so they scraped dust off the church walls and used that instead. That sounds more charming than likely, but it has been seriously proposed that marks are a by-product of scraping the stone for other purposes. In Germany the kind of cups found at Solihull are much more common, while grooves are less frequent. When these markings first came to the attention of historians in the 1870s, there were some people who said that they had been ground to produce medicinal dust. Others thought that they were made so that disease could be blown from the sufferer away into the hole; and others, that they were used by folk healers who rubbed the holes with grease, as a sort of transferred salve for sick bodies. Tradition evidently had many explanations for them, some sounding more like plausible guesses at what could have been done rather than personal testimony of what was. Other informants knew nothing about healing rituals and were confident instead that the grooves were made by the lazy dead, who had failed to attend church in their lifetimes and were now desperately clawing their way into sanctuary.[28]

Pilgrims were certainly encouraged to scrape up dust from the shrines they visited so that they could carry away a little holiness – a secondary relic – but this was usually ordinary household dust, although sometimes popular devotion went further and collected gratings from the stone itself. As a Gypsy said at the Saintes-Maries pilgrimage, 'That stone, monsieur, is the Saint's pillow and it is a magic stone. If you scratch it and mix some of the powder with water from the sacred well... a married woman who is barren, all she has to do is drink that lotion and she'll find herself big with twins, even though her husband is away at sea'.[29] At first sight this offers a convincing explanation for arrow sharpening marks, but it does not explain everything about them. It may not matter that marks are known to have been made in the sixteenth and seventeenth centuries, rather than the Middle Ages: after all, many popular customs involving parts of the church continued well into the nineteenth century.[30] But practicalities tell against the theory. Surely if dust was what people wanted, they would have scraped their knives along a flat or sloping stone and gathered it in a container, like someone brushing crumbs off a table. Cutting repeated grooves in a vertical wall would be the least effective way.

The purpose of mark-making was surely just that, to make marks: they are the intended end of what people were doing, not an accidental by-product of scraping, grinding, sharpening or anything else. Since we find them most often on churches, it is tempting to assume they were somehow religious or magical marks, but that may not necessarily follow: after all, there are also examples on secular buildings, and the corner of the church on which they appear is the least sacred part of the building. Porches were a half-secular space, used for meeting up and contracting parish business. If marks were a kind of prayer in stone, we would expect them to be more common inside than outside, and to cluster round the holy focus of the chancel. Instead they appear along the pathway to the door, at the porch, and on the wall beside it: exactly the places where people would be hanging around with time on their hands.

But for the historian of stories, it doesn't matter whether arrow sharpening marks were a little-known class of ritual markings or just the work of bored kids. They have acquired a second life through the popular tradition about bowmen preparing their arrowheads for target practice, and this repeated explanation is just as much of a cultural product as the marks themselves. But when was it first told?

A postcard from Devon, undated but c.1920, is captioned 'Marks due to Arrow Sharpening, Parish Church, Paignton'.[31] In 1917 Harry Gill wrote of 'the arrow-sharpening marks which abound on the south wall of many ancient churches' in Nottinghamshire, though he adds 'I know there is much diversity of opinion concerning the origin of these marks'.[32] A visitor to Swynnerton in Staffordshire was told that 'in ancient times, where the churches were built of sandstone, they sharpened their arrows on the walls or porches of the church, the holes made in sharpening them being plainly visible'. This was written in 1916, but the trip took place in 1871, so unless he updated his information from later guidebooks this would be the earliest record of the belief.[33] Certainly in 1883 grooves on Shropshire churches were explained this way and in 1882 those in Warwickshire were 'traditionally believed to have been produced by sharpening arrows'.[34]

Fig. 9. Paignton church, Devon.

But a myth does not come from nowhere: it needs characters and a setting to make it plausible. On the Continent marks of this kind have been found throughout Germany and the Netherlands, often on post-medieval buildings. The classic vertical deep boat-shaped scrapes into sandstone are mingled with round holes, taller scratches into limestone, and marks on brick.[35] As in

England, they are repeated along horizontal bands of the stonework, usually in conspicuous locations quite low on the outside walls. But nobody at these buildings talks about archers sharpening their arrows on churches because archery does not occupy the place in their national imaginary that it does in England. That patriotic past requires a particular blend of history and myth – myths which may have begun as history, but have long since been whittled down, isolated from criticism, and taken out of context. There is no doubt that from the fourteenth century onwards, the English war machine relied on archery units of a calibre which could not be matched by other European nations, and these were recruited from men who had been trained to the bow since childhood.[36] But it would be naïve to suppose that the laws of 1363 onwards, which commanded all able-bodied men to practice archery on Sundays and holy days, really translated into universal weekly sessions on the village green. The links between medieval legislation and real life were not that robust; in fact the laws had to be reissued over two centuries, precisely because most people took no notice of them. The centre of a village was in any case the last place where we would expect to find practice with lethal arms over a distance of 220 yards. Butts must have been set up on the common grazing, where they weathered away and were forgotten after the disuse of archery. The field-names in *butt*, brought into play at Shotwick and elsewhere to support the tale of the village archer, almost always refer instead to irregular blocks at the end of a medieval open-field system.[37]

Arrow sharpening marks are part of the lore that has snowballed around the real military success of English archery and its dependence on a picked corps of highly trained bowmen. But other traditions attribute grooves on stonework, not to archers making their arrows keen, but to soldiers in the wars of former times. The marks at Dunton Bassett are supposed to have been made by troops under the command of the Duke of Cumberland, sharpening their swords before they marched north to Culloden and the defeat of the Jacobites. Others, however, say that they were cut when Roundhead troops made the church their barracks in the Civil War. The grooves on the churchyard wall at Alveley are where Cromwell's men sharpened their swords. At Egmond in the same county, the marks on the church wall afterwards attributed to arrow sharpening were instead said to have been made by 'Cromwell's soldiers sharpening their swords'.[38]

At Barrow, also in Shropshire, grooves on a quoin or buttress are the work of Civil War soldiers (allegiance not stated). These are horizontal striations, possibly natural layering in the stone, and not arrow sharpening marks of the usual kind. In Lincolnshire it is the Royalists who are said to have sharpened their swords on the Winceby Stone before marching to battle.[39] In Somerset, where memories of the Monmouth Rising of 1686 have eclipsed all previous conflicts, they tell how stonework to the south of Chedzoy church was marked by rustics sharpening their swords and scythes before the last desperate fight at Sedgemoor.[40] The settlement called Whetstone at Friern Barnet in Middlesex got its name, so the locals said, from a large stone on the highway, used for that purpose by soldiers before the battle of Barnet in 1471.[41]

When it comes to sharpening, a groove in a wall would be as useless for swords as it is for arrows; on the other hand, a long blade can be given a cutting edge by pulling it sideways along hard stone, as in the old trick of whetting a carving knife on the back doorstep. When he wrote about arrow sharpening marks in Nottinghamshire, Harry Gill was careful to distinguish them from 'the broad-shaped depressions to be found on jambs of porches, on rims of fonts, and on parapets of bridges... These latter marks are obviously due to sharpening of blades'.[42] So, while the Whetstone tradition may not be true – the place was already going by that name a generation before the Wars of the Roses – it is not impossible. In 1806, at a time of rising tension between Napoleonic France and Berlin, some young Prussian officers did in fact sharpen their sabres on the stone steps of the French Embassy: an act of bravado which they were afterwards to regret.[43]

In the Welldean at Wooler, a slab of stone was pointed out as the block on which the inhabitants ground their swords and pikes when summoned to war. Given the bellicose conditions of life in old Northumberland, this is not unlikely.[44] But sword sharpening traditions easily fit themselves into a mythical past, especially outside England. Cloch na mBorradh, near Sixmilebridge in Co. Clare, was an isolated limestone erratic, the size of a haystack, resting on three smaller stones, and 'believed traditionally to have been placed there by Fian Mac Cumhall's warriors to serve them as a whetstone for their military weapons'.[45]

Generally beliefs in marks made by swords seem to be earlier than those which attribute them to arrows. The tradition at Cloch na mBorradh was recorded in 1855, but the stone had already featured in the thirteenth-century *Battle of Magh Leana*, where the marks are supposed to be dents made by an enemy army when Eoghan Mór was withdrawn by his *sí* mistress from the fray and replaced by a stone replica. And marks were being attributed to the Fianna a century earlier, when they appear in the *Acallam na Senórach*. Caílte is at the fort of Coscrach na Cét in Leinster where his host asks 'Why is this mighty stone here on the lawn called the Rock of the Weapons?', and the old hero answers 'This is the rock on which the Fían used to sharpen their weapons each year on the day of Samain and the edges that they put on them did not dull in battle, in skirmish, or in fighting'.[46]

If the legends of native England had endured as well as those of Gaelic Ireland, we might have a story to match that of Cloch na nArm at the mysterious Stone of the Sword, *sweordes stān*, recorded in a charter of 883 at Westbury on Trym in Gloucestershire.[47] As it is, only the name survives, bearing witness to an ancient tradition that linked stone monuments, especially grooved or cut monuments, with weapons and the days of old. This would bear fruit for later generations in the myth of the arrow sharpening mark: an inspiration to child and antiquarian alike, and a stumbling-block for sober historians.

Acknowledgements

I am grateful for photographs to John Billingsley (fig. 1), Brian Hoggard (fig. 4), Caroline Irwin (figs. 7 and 8) and the *Staffordshire Daily* (fig. 2). Fig. 3 was from Roger Griffith under Wikicommons (https://commons.wikimedia.org/wiki/File:Arrow_head_or_slate_pencil_sharpening_marks,_Stobo_Kirk.JPG) and fig. 6 from Philip Halling under Creative Commons (https://www.geograph.org.uk/photo/6634740). Fig. 5 I took myself.

Notes

1. http://www.shotwick.org.uk/church.html, accessed September 2021; site no longer current.
2. https://raggedrobinsnaturenotes.blogspot.com/2017/09/st-ethelburghas-church.html, accessed December 2021.
3. Pru Manning, 'Arrow sharpening marks' (2021): https://devonhistoricgraffiti.org.uk/news/, accessed December 2021; https://docbrown.info/docspics/suttonbank/sbspage17.htm, accessed December 2021.
4. https://historicengland.org.uk/listing/the-list/list-entry/1281625?section=comments-and-photos, accessed December 2021.
5. Manning, 'Arrow sharpening marks'; Michael Shapland, 'St Mary's, Broughton, Lincolnshire: a thegnly tower-nave in the late Anglo-Saxon landscape', *Archaeological Journal* 165 (2008) pp.471–519 at pp.479–81.
6. Brian McGarrigle, 'Stirling Castle's door and its mysterious grooves' (2015): https://www.scottishcastlesassociation.com/news/articles/stirling-castle-door.htm, accessed December 2021.
7. https://triskeleheritage.triskelepublishing.com/mediaeval-mythbusting-blog-10-arrow-stones/, accessed December 2021.
8. As recommended by Gaston de Foix in the fourteenth century: Erik Roth, *With a Bended Bow: Archery in Medieval and Renaissance Europe* (Stroud: Spellmount, 2012) p182.

9. London: British Library, MS Add 42130 f.147v.
10. Roth, *With a Bended Bow* pp.43–7.
11. Manning, 'Arrow sharpening marks'; https://www.weddingtoncastle.co.uk/st-nicolas-church.html, accessed December 2021.
12. There is a useful discussion of location by Howard Williams, 'The mysterious "arrow stones" of Shotwick' (2021): https://howardwilliamsblog.wordpress.com/2021/11/19/the-mysterious-arrow-stones-of-shotwick/, accessed December 2021.
13. https://twitter.com/baddileyram/status/1101982881646342145, accessed December 2021.
14. https://www.flickr.com/photos/nekoglyph/28189289280, accessed December 2021.
15. https://rakinglight.co.uk/uk/st-mary-the-virgin-alveley-shropshire/, accessed December 2021; taken from Pamela Thom-Rowe, 'Arrow/sword sharpening marks, Shropshire' (2021), which is no longer online.
16. https://www.leicestershirechurches.co.uk/dunton-bassett-church-all-saints/, accessed December 2021.
17. Harry Gill, 'The church porches and doorways of Nottinghamshire', *Tr. of the Thoroton Soc.* 21 (1917) pp.1–45 at p.9.
18. Shapland, 'St Mary's, Broughton'.
19. http://sussexhistoryforum.co.uk/index.php?PHPSESSID=knih3dfr2elfc2b12f933eunq1&topic=8926.0, accessed December 2021.
20. 'Suckley church through the ages' (2006): https://media.acny.uk/media/venues/page/attachment/2020/10/Discover_the_hidden_treasures_of_Suckley_Church.final_sma_qfRuXxI.pdf.
21. McGarrigle, 'Stirling Castle'.
22. https://www.flickr.com/photos/barryslemmings/2056059024/in/photostream/, accessed December 2021.
23. Gill, 'The church porches and doorways of Nottinghamshire'.
24. https://raggedrobinsnaturenotes.blogspot.com/2016/07/the-parish-church-of-st-alphege-solihull.html, accessed December 2021.
25. Jacqueline Cameron, *Kenilworth through Time* (Stroud: Amberley, 2010).
26. Wilfrid Bonser, 'Letter to the editor', *Folklore* 69 (1958) p.204.
27. Charles Godfrey Leland, 'Marks on ancient monuments', *Folk-Lore* 8 (1897) pp.86–7.
28. Charles Rau, *Observations on Cup-Shaped and other Lapidarian Sculpture in the Old World and in America*, Contributions to North American Ethnology 5 (Washington WA: Government Printing Office, 1881) pp.87–9.
29. Katharine Esty, *The Gypsies, Wanderers in Time* (New York: Meredith Press, 1969) p.84.

30. Examples are collected in Jan Weertz, Els Weertz and Christopher Duffin, 'Possible sources of therapeutic stone powder from North West Europe', *Pharmaceutical Historian* 44 (2014) pp27–32, but the connection with marks remains tentative.
31. Seen on Ebay, August 2021; no longer online.
32. Gill, 'The church porches and doorways of Nottinghamshire'.
33. Robert Naylor, *From John O'Groat's to Land's End* (Privately published, 1916) p.364.
34. Charlotte Burne and Georgina Jackson, *Shropshire Folk-Lore: A Sheaf of Gleanings* (London: Trübner, 1883) p.94; William Andrews, 'Cup and circle markings on church walls in Warwickshire and the neighbourhood', *Archaeological Journal* 46 (1889) pp.156–8 at p.156.
35. Peter Schels, *Schabespuren auf Stein (Rillen und Näpfchen): Fakten, Überlegungen, Funde* (Privately published, 2007); Judith Schuyf, *Heidense heiligddomen: Zichtbare sporen van een verloren verleden* (Utrecht: Uitgeverij Omniboek, 2019) pp.210–14. I owe these references to the generosity of Marc Robben.
36. Douglas Allen and Peter Leeson, 'Institutionally constrained technology adoption: resolving the longbow puzzle', *Journal of Law and Economics* 58 (2015) pp.683–715.
37. Paul Cavill, *A New Dictionary of English Field-Names* (Nottingham: English Place-Name Society, 2018) p.55.
38. Burne and Jackson, *Shropshire Folk-Lore* p.94.
39. Ethel Rudkin, 'Lincolnshire folklore: III', *Folk-Lore* 45 (1934) pp.144–57 at p.155.
40. 'Afternoon excursion: I', *Proceedings of the Somerset Archaeology and Natural History Society* 23 (1877) pp.35–7.
41. John Gover, Allen Mawer and Frank Stenton, *The Place-Names of Middlesex apart from the City of London*, Survey of English Place-Names 18 (Cambridge: English Place-Name Society, 1942) pp.100–1.
42. Gill, 'The church porches and doorways of Nottinghamshire'.
43. Andrew Roberts, *Napoleon the Great* (London: Penguin, 2014) p.411.
44. James Hardy, 'On Langleyford Vale and the Cheviots', *History of the Berwickshire Naturalists' Club* 6 (1869–72) pp.353–75 at p.355.
45. Eugene O'Curry, *Cáth Mhuighe Léana, or, the Battle of Magh Leana* (Dublin: Celtic Society, 1855) pp.30–1; by 1899 the stone was called Cloughmornia or Cloughlea, but with the same tradition – Thomas Westropp, 'A folklore survey of County Clare: VIII', *Folk-Lore* 23 (1912) pp.88–94 at p.90
46. *Tales of the Elders of Ireland*, tr Ann Dooley and Harry Roe (Oxford: Oxford University Press, 1999) p.125. Conor Newman has interpreted other significant grooves on Irish standing stones in the light of this tradition: 'The

sword in the stone: previously unrecognized archaeological evidence of ceremonies of the later Iron Age and early medieval period', in *Relics of Old Decency: Archaeological Studies in Late Prehistory* ed Gabriel Cooney *et al* (Dublin: Wordwell, 2009) pp.425-36.

47. Albert Hugh Smith, *The Place-Names of Gloucestershire*, Survey of English Place-Names 38-41 (Cambridge: English Place-Name Society, 1964-5) 3 p.145.

Hiding in Plain Sight: Pagan protection rituals in popular celebrations of St Brigid in Ireland

Jeannine Woods

Despite the growing secularisation of Irish society in recent decades, St Brigid's Day/ *Lá Fhéile Bríde* is still celebrated in contemporary Ireland as a popular festival with cultural as well as religious importance. Some of the traditional rituals pertaining to the feast are still practised and indeed have seen a revival in recent years. It shows the continued popular attachment to the figure of Brigid that, when a new bank holiday in Ireland was proposed to recognise the efforts of healthcare workers and sacrifices of the population in the Covid 19 pandemic, there were calls for the new holiday to be established on St Brigid's Day on February 1st; the government duly announced that the country's new bank holiday will fall on the Monday closest to the feast day. There is a great deal of information on the traditional rituals of Brigid's Day in the archives of the National Folklore Collection, much of it in response to a questionnaire issued specifically on 'The Feast of St Brigid' by the Irish Folklore Commission in 1942. Accounts collected between the 1930s and the 1960s show that some or all of the ritual practices were widespread throughout Ireland well into the twentieth century: some accounts describe practices that were current in the community while others detail those remembered but no longer practised. Unsurprisingly, these traditions tended to live on in rural areas, and were often strongest in *Gaeltacht* communities where Irish is the primary language of the community. Although the feast day is associated with Brigid the saint of the church calendar, the roles of the *Brat Bríde*/ Brigid's Cloak, the *Cros Bhríde*/ Brigid's Cross, the *Brídeog*/ Biddy and the *Crios Bríde*/ Brigid's Belt as protective and curative ritual objects suggest what 'hides in plain sight' – that traditional popular practices were directed at least as much towards Brigid the pre-Christian goddess as towards the Christian saint.

Brigid's dual identity

While Brigid is generally represented as a saint who lived in the fifth century, medieval scholars and scholars of mythology have long noted a pagan goddess Brigid, important not only in Ireland but throughout Gaul and Britain. The archaeological record suggests that this goddess was found throughout Europe; Marija Gimbutas asserted that 'Brigid is an Old European goddess consigned to the guise of a Christian saint. Remove the guise and you will see the mistress of nature, an incarnation of cosmic life-giving energy, the owner of life water in wells and springs, the bestower of human, animal and plant life'.[1] In the Irish cult of St Brigid, scholars have highlighted the overarching presence of the pre-Christian goddess within accounts and beliefs surrounding the saint, MacCana noting that 'if the historical element in the legend of St Brighid is slight, the mythological element is correspondingly extensive, and it is clear beyond question that the saint has usurped the role of the goddess and much of her mythological tradition'.[2]

The medieval accounts of Brigid as goddess and as saint demonstrate overlap between the two figures. The eighth-century text *Sanas Cormaic* (Cormac's Glossary), an etymological and explanatory glossary of Irish words, contains the following entry:

> Brigit, that is to say, the poetess, daughter of the Dagda. This is Brigit the female sage, or woman of wisdom, i.e. Brigit the goddess whom poets used to worship, because very great and very famous was her protecting care. It is therefore they call the goddess of poets by this name. Whose sisters were Brigit the woman of leechcraft and Brigit the woman of smith work; from these names Irishmen used to give the name Brigit to almost every goddess. Brigit, *breo-aighit/ breo-shaigit* 'a fiery arrow'.[3]

The editor's note following this entry asserts that Brigid 'is certainly (as Siegfried thought) connected with the O.Celtic goddess-name Brigantia and possibly with the Skr. Bhraspati and O.Norse Bragi'.[4] The Dagda (meaning 'good god') is a important god of the Tuatha Dé Danann, a mythological group of supernatural beings who form most of the pre-Christian Celtic pantheon and who dwell in the otherworld. In keeping with the pattern found in relation to Celtic goddess figures, Brigid is described here as a threefold goddess. The medieval text *Lebor Gabála Érenn* (The Book of Invasions) also refers to Brigid as a poetess and daughter of the Dagda. It states that she has two oxen and a boar and that these animals would cry out to warn of danger, suggesting that Brigid was a guardian goddess of domesticated animals.[5]

Medieval Irish literature contains a number of lives of St Brigid; the earliest, written by the monk Cogitosus, dates to the 7th century. These all contain elements that clearly relate to the pre-Christian goddess. The lives tell how Brigid's mother, Broicseach, gave birth to her as she was entering a house carrying a bucket of buttermilk; she had one foot inside the threshold and one foot outside the threshold when Brigid was born. This motif aligns St Brigid with pre-Christian cosmologies in which otherworld figures are associated with literal thresholds as well as with threshold points in the calendar. Accounts of the life of Brigid tell that everything under her care flourished; many of the miracles attributed to the saint involve the miraculous production of food, including extraordinary amounts of milk given by her cattle. The saint, like the goddess, is associated with bounty; it is particularly interesting to note that a popular folkloric tale associates Goibniu, a member of the Tuatha Dé Danann and the god of smithing, with a prize cow known as *Glas Gaibhnenn* which yielded profuse quantities of milk.

Accounts of the life of St Brigid also associate her with fire. The biographies tell that the monastery founded by Brigid at Kildare boasted a perpetual fire, tended by the saint and her nuns. Writing seven centuries after the founding of the monastery, Giraldus Cambrensis recorded the following information on the perpetual fire in his *Topographia Hibernica*:

> The fire is surrounded by a hedge, made of stakes and brushwood, and forming a circle, within which no male can enter; and if any one would presume to enter, which has sometimes been attempted by rash men, he will not escape the divine vengeance. Moreover, it is only lawful for women to blow the fire, fanning it or using bellows only, and not with their breath.[6]

The institution of a perpetual fire, and the female power surrounding its origin and maintenance, are unusual in a Christian context and suggest vestiges of a female goddess cult; it has been speculated that Kildare, Irish *Cill Dara* 'church of the oak', may have been an earlier druidic site. We have already seen the pre-Christian figure of Brigid connected with fire both in her association with smithing and in the interpretation of her name by Cormac's Glossary as 'fiery arrow'; variations of the ritual Brigid's Cross, detailed below, also suggest an association with the sun. Links between perpetual fire and a powerful female divinity are strongly suggested by Ó Duinn's research into connections between Brigid and the Celto-Roman goddess Sulis-Minerva, whose temple in Bath also claimed a tradition of a perpetual fire:

> Professor McCone speaks of this theory concerning Minerva and the boiling medicinal well at Bath (*Aquae Sulis*): 'It thus seems quite likely that the Bath cult and its Christianised Kildare counterpart related ultimately to the same goddess, variously known as "Briganti", "exalted one", or "Sul" "sun" cognate with Latin "sol", Welsh "haul", semantically shifted Irish "súil" "eye" and so on. At all events, the pagan Brigit's association with sun and fire seems to be beyond reasonable doubt'.[7]

Brigid's subversion of the patriarchal gender norms of Christianity and her singular power and status as a female saint are most evident in her ordination as a bishop. One account of her ordination is found in the ninth-century biography *Bethu Brigte*. According to this account, Bishop Mel, while ordaining Brigid as a nun, read the wrong prayers, resulting in her ordination as a bishop. When asked why he had read the incorrect prayers, the bishop proclaimed that the Holy Spirit had taken the matter out of his hands: 'The bishop being intoxicated with the grace of God there did not recognize what he was reciting from his book, for he consecrated Brigit with the orders of a Bishop. "This virgin alone in Ireland", said Mel, "will hold the Episcopal ordination". While she was being consecrated a fiery column ascended from her head'.[8]

Lá Fhéile Bríde/ The Feast of Brigid

St Brigid's feast day falls on February 1st; in the pre-Christian calendar, this is the festival of *Imbolc*, which along with *Bealtaine*, *Lúnasa* and *Samhain*, makes up the four seasonal festivals of the year. It marks the beginning of spring, and is associated with fertility, the resurgence of growth and bounty after winter, and in agriculture, the first sowing of crops and the birth of farm animals. Cormac's Glossary defines *Imbolc* (*Óimelc* in old Irish) thus: '*Ói* i.e. a sheep...*Óimelc* ("beginning of spring") i.e. *ói-melg* 'ewe-milk', i.e. that is the time the sheep's milk comes; *melg*, i.e. milk, because it is milked'.[9] The term may translate literally as 'in the belly (womb)'; in both cases it is clearly closely associated with fertility, (re)birth and new life. In pre-Christian cosmology, the seasonal festivals were seen as liminal periods, when the veil between this world and the otherworld thinned and otherworld figures, including gods and goddesses, were likely to enter this world. Such periods were viewed as magical, but might also be precarious, given the ability of otherworldly beings in this world to exert a benign or malign influence on humans and on human life. Such precarity is much in evidence in traditional popular beliefs and practices in relation to *Oíche Shamhna* (Hallowe'en), some of which were concerned with protecting the human community from malign otherworldly encounters and influences. The practices and associated objects explored here demonstrate their pre-Christian origins, yet suggest that the influence of the goddess Brigid during the festival of *Imbolc* was unambiguously benevolent and protective.

Many of the traditional popular rituals and practices took place on or after sunset on the eve of St Brigid's Day, in keeping with pre-Christian practices of beginning celebrations after sunset on the eve of a festival, as seen in the celebration of Hallowe'en. Several of the objects or the materials from which they were made were gathered at this time: the objects obtained their power by being placed outside the house or on its threshold. Objects obtained their power from Brigid herself, who walked the earth on Brigid's Eve and blessed objects as she passed. An account of Brigid's visit collected in 1942 gives a detailed picture of popular beliefs and about Brigid, and underscores some of their pre-Christian elements:

> On the eve of St. Brigid a sheaf of rushes (green) was placed on the doorway or flagstone of the door on the outside on which St. Brigid would kneel when she and St. Brigid's cow visited during the night. St. Brigid would kneel on the rushes and pray that God might bless the house and its occupants. Also it was a custom to tie the St. Brigid's ribbon [a variant of *Brat Bríde/* Brigid's Cloak] on the latch of the door outside and this also she blessed when she blessed the house, the people in it and especially the dairy and cattle. No house was locked on the night of St. Brigid's Eve but the door was kept on the latch. When St. Brigid came along she drove a white cow which was known as St. Brigid's cow but that had a special name in Irish ... The old people used to say 'St Brigid and her cow will come around tonight'. Usually milk is very scarce in January, but the old people used to say during the month when they heard anyone complaining of the scarcity of milk; 'It won't be scarce very long now as St. Brigid and her white cow will be coming around.[10]

The return of Brigid is itself a reflection of pre-Christian beliefs and cosmologies, where figures enter this world from the otherworld. As Seán Ó Duinn notes:

> It must be asked, if it is the normal practice for a Christian saint to return to earth on his or her feastday? The answer is quite clear – it is not the custom for a saint to come back on this occasion. The annual return of a saint is not part of the tradition of the Catholic Church ... The return of Brigid from the Otherworld at *Imbolc* may be situated within this context of the breakdown of barriers and the visitation of pre-Christian deities at sacred seasons of the agricultural year.[11]

Gathering of Rushes and *Gnás na Tairsí/* The Threshold Rite
Brigit's Eve saw the gathering of rushes, which were left on the threshold of the house for blessing by Brigid and brought in later in the evening to make crosses and other ritual objects associated with the festival. In some parts of

the country, a dish of salt was left on the doorstep and afterwards used to cure sore throats.[12] It was also common practice to leave a sheaf of oats or corn (or, in areas where the potato had become the primary crop, a potato set) on the threshold for blessing by Brigid; the sheaf or set would be added to the year's planting to ensure a good crop later in the year.[13] The Threshold Rite involved a ritual meal comprising foods with rich in milk and butter, such as *brúitín/* poundies (potatoes mashed with large quantities of butter and milk). The importance of milk and dairy produce in the context of Brigid's feast has already been seen to be associated with lactation and therefore with new life. Ó Catháin posits that butter is particularly significant here:

> Butter [is] the product of churning. The act of churning, an imitation of the act of sexual intercourse, represents creation. The appearance of the butter may be taken to stand for the arrival of the much hoped for product of that sexual union. The implements used for churning also carry their own obvious sexual message: the churn and dash representing the female and male sexual organs respectively.[14]

Before the meal was eaten, a member of the household (either the man of the house or a daughter, depending on the region) went outside, gathered the rushes left on the doorstep (in some cases covering them with a garment) making the rush bundle into a *Brídeog/* Biddy effigy as discussed below. The person carrying the effigy circumambulated the house three times in a sunwise direction, before calling to those within:

> Go on your knees, Open your eyes, And admit Brigid!

Those within would give the ceremonial response:

> Welcome! Welcome! Welcome to the noble/ holy woman![15]

The *Brídeog* was carefully placed under the table or under the pot containing the supper; after the meal was eaten, the family used the rushes to make Brigid's Crosses. The invocation of Brigid in the sphere of fecundity and rebirth is evident in the various elements of this rite; her power and protection is brought across the threshold through the effigy of the *Brídeog*, made here of rushes blessed by Brigid, while the ritual of travelling sunwise around the house three times before entering echoes the pre-Christian *Cor Deiseal* procession around a sacred object a set number of times (usually three times or nine, both being sacred numbers), following the course of the sun to invoke luck and prosperity.[16]

Brat Bríde/ Brigid's Cloak

Associations with fertility, protection and with the curing of illness are also seen in relation to the *Brat Bríde*. A piece of fabric or clothing was left outside near the threshold of the house after sunset on Brigid's Eve for blessing by Brigid and taken in before sunrise. Various accounts within the archives of the National Folklore Collection detail the use of the *Brat* as a cure for headaches, toothaches, and for sore eyes.[17] It was also used as a cure for ringworm in cattle. In some areas, items of clothing belonging to each member of the family were left out overnight to impart Brigid's protection to the wearers, while in other areas the *Brat* was cut and pieces of it were sewn into clothing for the same purpose. Brigid's protection was especially important for those engaged in dangerous work; Danaher notes that it was 'worn if the wearer was engaged in any hazardous pursuit or journey to a distant place; it is often thus worn by fishermen and many stories are told of how this fishing boat or that escaped the perils of the sea and storm because one of the crew wore the *Brat Bríde*'.[18]

The *Brat* was also directly associated with human fertility and birthing. Some accounts detail its power to cure infertility in women, and midwives or 'handy women' used the *Brat* to aid with labour and safe delivery. One account tells that a local midwife

> had one of those *brait* … she was a handy woman and she used to place it on the head of any woman sick in childbed. I was very bad when I was having my first child and Neilí placed the *Cochall Bríde* [another term for the *Brat Bríde*] on my head and I got relief.[19]

The power of the *Brat* also underlines Brigid's association with cattle. It was used to aid with calving, as detailed in the following account:

> There was a poor old woman going around this place long ago and she had a shawl which was a *Bratach Bríde* of fourteen-years' standing and any request she made in the name of the shawl, she was granted it. She went into one of the houses here once. There was a cow tethered at the lower end of the house, about to calve, but the calf wasn't coming and appeared unlikely to do so and the cow seemed doomed. The poor woman enquired – 'Are you not doing any good?' They said they weren't. 'Well, go down again,' says she, 'and try her once more'. The men went down and tackled the cow again.

> And the old woman shook the shawl over the cow and went down on her two knees there and began to pray to Brigit the Holy Woman. It wasn't ten minutes till the cow was alright.[20]

The *Brat* was further used to aid cattle postpartum and to protect the offspring:

> *Brat Bríde* was supposed to be an infallible cure for cows after calving that had kept what they call here 'the clanins' – the afterbirth. They placed it on the hindquarters of the cow and it got alright. Always when a cow calves on that particular farm, the *Brat* is spread over the cow's back. This brings good luck and the cow will have an abundance of milk and the calf will thrive marvellous.[21]

Cros Bhríde/ Brigid's Cross

Brigid's Cross, traditionally made of rushes left on the threshold for blessing by Brigid, is the most enduring of the popular ritual objects associated with the festival, familiar even to those who otherwise have little or no knowledge of the traditional celebrations. Instructions on making a Brigid's Cross are widely available (including instructional videos on Youtube) and the making of crosses on Brigid's Day is now popular both in Ireland and in many areas around the world. Crosses were traditionally made by family members on Brigid's Eve after the ceremonial meal. While the most commonly recognised form of Brigid's Cross is probably the four-armed cross – it was adopted as the original logo of Ireland's national broadcaster Raidió Éireann, later RTÉ, which doubtless helped to boost its profile – several forms of the cross exist, with one or more types associated with various regions of the country. The interwoven cross and the type known as Brigid's Bow (*Bogha Bríde*) correspond formally with the Christian cross. The three-armed and four-armed cross, however, diverge significantly from the Christian form. The four-armed cross corresponds with the ancient symbol of the swastika: this association is also seen in the inscription of a swastika on a stone from the early Christian period located near St Brigid's Well at Cliffoney in Co. Sligo.[22] The three-armed cross may be associated with the triskele, another symbol of great antiquity found in many cultures including that of Neolithic Ireland where it was carved on

Fig. 1. (previous page) Woman churning, Gorumna Island, Co. Galway, 1930s.

Fig. 2. (below) St Brigid's Cross types – 1, interwoven cross; 2, diamond/ lozenge cross; 3, three-armed cross; 4, diamond/ lozenge cross variant; 5, four-armed/ swastika cross; 6, Bogha Bríde/ St. Brigid's Bow.

kerbstones at Newgrange and elsewhere. Ó Duinn argues that both the three- and four-armed cross types suggest a wheel in motion and may symbolise the movement of the sun as winter moves into spring.[23]

The diamond or lozenge shape is the most widely distributed form of Brigid's Cross, found in all of the Irish provinces. Variations are a stand-alone diamond or a large, central diamond with smaller diamonds placed above the points of the central diamond. Fieldwork by the archaeologist Marija Gimbutas has revealed the diamond or lozenge motif to be widely associated with a goddess figure across Europe and Asia as far back as 7000–6000 BC. Gimbutas concludes that the motif is associated with growth and fertility:

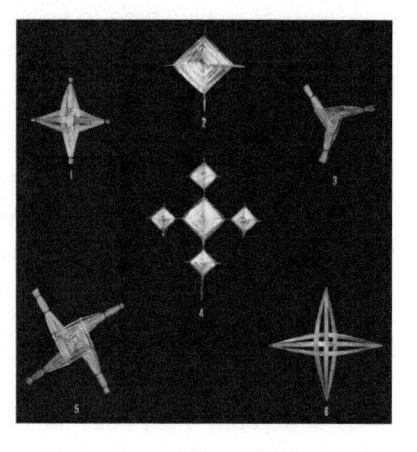

> The lozenge and triangle with one or more dots on shrine walls, vases, seals, and typically on the pregnant belly or other parts of the Pregnant Goddess, starting in the 7th millennium BC. In origin, both glyphs are probably schematized configurations of the vulva and the pubic triangle and relate to the life-source. The dots perhaps represent the seed inside the womb or field ... The lozenge with a dot in four corners may denote 'planting in all four directions', a concept still extant in European folk belief.[24]

The lozenge or diamond motif is not confined to the Brigid's Cross in Ireland; it is also found at the megalithic monuments at Newgrange, Knowth and Fourknocks, as well as early Christian ecclesiastical sites including Kildare Cathedral, Killaloe Cathedral and the High Cross of Moone, Co. Kildare. It has been suggested that the motif forms the basis of the pattern of the *báinín* or *geansaí Árann* (Aran jumper), a traditional style of knitted pullover associated with the Aran Islands, Co. Galway.[25]

Brigid's Crosses were placed in the rafters of the house and of outhouses as to protect human and animal inhabitants against 'fire, famine and fever'. The cross was generally replaced each year, or a new one placed over the crosses of previous years. While the customary location for the cross was within the house and outhouses, it could be placed in a basket of seeds and carried into the fields at sowing time to ensure the fertility of the new season's crops.[26] It was customary to give a gift of a Brigid's Cross to those moving into a new house to protect the home, and to a newly wedded couple to aid their success in starting a family.

Brídeog & Brídeoga/ The Biddy Effigy and Procession

The *Brídeog* or Biddy effigy was part of the Threshold Rite but was also central to the celebrations that moved beyond the family homestead. Brigid's Eve traditionally saw a procession around the community of 'Biddies' or 'Biddy Boys' (known as *Brídeoga* in Irish), with boys and young men (less often girls or mixed groups of young people) carrying a Biddy effigy to pay visits to households in the community, where they were given gifts of food and, later, money in the name of Brigid. The following account details the practice in Crumlin, Co. Galway:

Fig. 3. Brídeog/ Biddy effigy: Cill Ghobnait, Co. Kerry, 1974.

> Groups of boys go from house to house with 'Brídeoga' on that night. A *Brídeog* is a small effigy of St. Brigid. It is often made from straw and rags and each group has one. The boys put on old clothes and masks and people don't know who they are. Every group has a musical instrument and they do some dancing in each house. They also wear belts made of straw. One of those is called '*Crios Bríde*/ Brigid's Belt'. The people give them a little money (sixpence or threepence in each house). In times gone by they were given eggs.[27]

An element of disguise features here, as it did in celebrations of *Oíche Shamhna*; disguise was a means of protection against kidnapping by the *slua sí*/ fairy folk, inhabitants of the otherworld who came into the human world at liminal periods and who on departing might take humans back to their domain. The adoption of disguise also acts out ritual liminality, an aspect of these customs detailed by Arnold Van Gennep and developed by Victor Turner, in which day-to-day practices and conventions are often inverted.[28] Such an inversion is seen in the gender switching employed in some regions for the disguise of the Biddy group:

> The *Brídeog* procession from house to house was and still is held on the eve of the feast ... Boys dress in girls' clothes as a rule and vice versa. Long ago a turnip was used to represent the head of the *Brídeog* ... A stick was inserted into the turnip to lend body to the *Brídeog* and to make it easy to carry ... They are all disguised and are led by the one carrying the *Brídeog* who is first to enter a house.[29]

The stick which formed the body of the *Brídeog* was very often a churn dash, which Ó Catháin argues is significant given the symbolic significance of this tool:

> The phallic qualities of the loinid [churn dash] are also highlighted in a setting other than churning ... namely its function as the central axis around which the doll image of Brigit, the *brídeog* (a word which also means bride) is constructed. We may also note that the act of calling for admission in Brigit's name, while this shaft is thrust through the door opening, functions within the tradition as an alternative to the action of the man of the house in seeking entry, armed with a sheaf or straw [as part of the Threshold Rite] – his *brídeog*, as it were – and it must be seen as an exact parallel to it.[30]

Fig. 4. Biddy Boys: Cill Ghobnait, Co. Kerry, 1974.

As a ritual practice extending beyond the family homestead, the Biddy procession sought to invoke protection and to ensure abundant food supply for the community, through reciprocal exchanges performed in the name of Brigid. It protected the luck of the house and ensured ample butter production throughout the year. This theme of abundant food and dairy supply is made explicit in a report from Mayo: after gifts were given by the household to the group, the Biddies' response was 'If you ever be

Fig. 5. Biddy Boy and Brídeog/Biddy: Cill Ghobnait, Co. Kerry, 1974.

short Brigid will give you some', at which point the Biddies were given a drink of milk, and after drinking they responded 'May none of your cows die during the year'.[31]

Crios Bríde/ Brigid's Belt

Ritual practices involving the *Crios Bríde/* Brigid's Belt were particular to the West of Ireland. The *Crios* or Belt was made from a large straw rope joined at either end to form a circle, with three or four Brigid's crosses woven into it. Accounts of the ritual use of the *Crios* show some variation: in some regions it was brought from house to house by the Biddy troupe (as seen in the description from Crumlin, Co. Galway, above), but in other areas the custom was separate from the *Brídeog* procession, sometimes practiced by individual families rather than a community. The ceremony involved ritual passing three times through the belt, kissing one of the crosses each time, and emerging right foot foremost. All members of the household would take part, with women often being the first to perform the rite. Children who were too small to do this themselves were passed through the *Crios* to obtain its blessings. It's possible that the *Crios* rite may derive from a rite symbolising the journey of birth: Ó Catháin notes that 'passing through' has been recognised as an archaic and widespread remedy within folk medicine in various parts of the world.[32] The ritual protected its participants from illness: one account from Ros Muc in Co. Galway describes how the ceremony was extended to cattle by hanging a large *Crios* on the door of the cow house so that cattle passing through the door would also receive the protection of Brigid.[33]

Holy wells and patterns associated with Brigid

Holy wells are numerous in Ireland; most are associated with a particular saint and many serve as the site of patterns on the saint's feast day or another date. A pattern involves ritual rounds of a sacred site, with prayers said in a particular sequence to invoke blessings and healing. Traditionally, pattern days were served as major social events, drawing large gatherings in a festival-like atmosphere. Patterns were sometimes denounced by the Catholic church and by middle-

Fig. 6. Crios Bríde/ Brigid's Belt Rite at St Brigid's Well, Liscannor, Co. Clare, 2016.

and upper-class observers in Ireland as 'uncivilised' pagan practices, but nonetheless endured in many areas.[34] A commentary of the early nineteenth century by one such observer of patterns to various holy wells, including Brigid's, gives a flavour both of 'outsider' and 'insider' perspectives on the practice:

> *I have often inquired of your tenants what they themselves thought of their pilgrimages to the wells of Kill-Aracht, Tobbar Brighde, Tobbar Muir, near Elphin, Moor, near Castlereagh, where multitudes annually assembled to celebrate what they, in broken English, termed Patterns (Patron's days); and when I pressed a very old man, Owen Hester, to state what possible advantage they expected to derive from the singular custom of frequenting in particular such wells as were contiguous to an old blasted oak, or an upright hewn stone, and what the meaning was of the yet more singular custom of sticking rags on the branches of such trees and spitting on them, his answer, and the answer of the oldest men, was that their ancestors always did it, and that it was a preservation against Geasa Draoidecht, i.e., the sorceries of the Druids, and that their cattle were preserved by it from infectious disorders; that the daoini maithe, i.e., the fairies, were kept in good humour by it; and so thoroughly persuaded were they of the sanctity of these Pagan practices that they would travel bareheaded and barefooted from ten to twenty miles for the purpose of crawling on their knees round these wells, upright stones, and oak trees, westward, as the sun travels, some three times, some six, some nine, and so on in uneven numbers until their voluntary penances were completely fulfilled.*[35]

Holy wells throughout Ireland are dedicated to Brigid; they cure conditions such as infertility, eye ailments, toothache and offer general healing. One such well is in Liscannor, Co. Clare. The pattern day of this site occurs at Lúnasa at the beginning of August, but

Fig. 7. Offerings at St Brigid's Well, Liscannor, Co. Clare, 2008.

the well has traditionally featured in celebrations of Brigid's Day; in recent years, the local parish priest Fr Denis Crosby has performed a feast day mass at the spring which includes traditional popular ritual celebrations such as Crios Bríde, while many of those who attend complete ritual rounds of the well on the day. Interest in and visits to the well in Liscannor have further increased as the result of its inclusion in tourist guides and blogs. Many visitors to the well follow the established practice of leaving personal objects at the site to invoke blessing or healing, with the result that the well is now home to a huge amount of such materials.

Conclusion

The twin identities of Brigid, goddess and saint, pervade the popular rituals that celebrate her feast day, several of which survived into the 1980s and beyond, while the making and use of Brigid's Crosses has been continuously observed to the present; some of the other practices and objects have been revived in recent years. Continued observance of such popular practices owes much to the importance ascribed by communities to the honouring of tradition. While these tributes to Brigid were framed as honouring the Christian saint, participants were not unaware of their dual cosmological focus. Such awareness, seen in the words of Owen Hester in relation to patterns in the early 19th century, has often been expressed when people talk about popular ritual practices which display pre-Christian elements. When it comes to Brigid, for example, a Donegal storyteller relating a tale in the late 1930s explained that 'There were two Saint Brigids. There was Saint Brigid in Kildare, but this is Saint Brigid from this place'.[36] Unlike many other popular ritual traditions, however, the syncretic representation of Saint Brigid in ecclesiastical manuscripts from the medieval period gave Christian sanction to popular understandings and practices encompassing both saint and goddess, and facilitated their continued practice without denunciation or suppression by the Church. It is no small paradox that popular rites celebrating a pre-Christian goddess have successfully endured in Ireland not despite but because of the partial refiguration of Brigid as a Christian saint.

Acknowledgements

Figs. 1 to 5 are from the Photographic Collection, National Folklore Collection, UCD, respectively H032.06.00001, B105.01.00003, H032.18.00021, H032.18.00002 and H032.18.00009. Fig. 6 is from Tony Kirby (https://www.heartofburrenwalks.com/brigid-and-harry) and fig. 7 from Mark Waters, 'St Brigid's Well, Liscannor, County Clare' via Flickr 3243151713.

Notes

1. Marija Gimbutas, The Living Goddesses (California: University of California Press, 2001) p.184.
2. Proinsias MacCana, Celtic Mythology (London: Hamlyn, 1970) p.34.

3. Whitley Stokes and John O'Donovan, eds., Sanais Cormaic/ Cormac's Glossary (Calcutta: Irish Archaeological and Celtic Society, 1868) p.23.
4. Stokes and O'Donovan, Sanas Cormaic p.23.
5. John Ó Ríordáin, Early Irish Saints (Dublin: Columba Press, 1991) p.25
6. Giraldus Cambrensis, ed. Thomas Wright, The Historical Works of Giraldus Cambrensis (London: George Bell & Sons, 1894) pp.96–7.
7. Seán Ó Duinn, The Rites of Brigid: Goddess and Saint (Dublin: Columba Press, 2013) pp.64–5 citing Kim McCone, Pagan Past and Christian Present in Early Irish Literature (Maynooth: An Sagart, 1990).
8. Donnchadh Ó hAodha, ed., Bethu Brigte, CELT Project, UCC: http://publish.ucc.ie/celt/document/T201002 (accessed December 2021).
9. Stokes and O'Donovan, Sanas Cormaic p.127.
10. Irish Folklore Commission (IFC) 899: 259–65.
11. Ó Duinn, The Rites of Brigid pp.38, 45.
12. Johnny Dillon, 'St. Brigid and her powerful cultural heritage', RTÉ website (30 January 2020): https://www.rte.ie/gaeilge/2019/0110/1022457-st-brigid-and-her-powerful-cultural-heritage/ (accessed December 2021).
13. See IFC 902: 108; Kevin Danaher, The Year in Ireland (Dublin: Mercier, 1972) pp.13–19.
14. Séamas Ó Catháin, The Festival of Brigit: Celtic Goddess and Holy Woman (Dublin: DBA, 1995) pp.14–15.
15. Ó Catháin, The Festival of Brigit p.42; see also Ó Duinn, The Rites of Brigid pp.101–2; Danaher, The Year in Ireland pp.18–21.
16. Ó Duinn, The Rites of Brigid pp.100–101.
17. IFC 899: 263–4; IFC 902: 46; IFC 902: 285–6.
18. Danaher, The Year in Ireland p.33.
19. IFC 899: 108 (translation from Irish).
20. IFC 904: 67–9, tr. in Ó Catháin, The Festival of Brigit p.3.
21. IFC 902: 254.
22. Ó Catháin, The Festival of Brigit p.15.
23. Ó Duinn, The Rites of Brigid pp.121–2.
24. 'The earth fertility of Old Europe', Dialogues d'histoire ancienne 13 (1987) pp.11–69 at pp.14–15.
25. Pádraig Ó Síocháin, Aran: Islands of Legend (third edition, Dublin: Foilsiúcháin Éireann, 1967) pp.179, 181.
26. Seán Ó Súilleabháin, Lá Fhéile Bríde (Dublin: Irish Folklore Commission, 1977) p.4; Danaher, The Year in Ireland p.25.
27. The Schools' Collection, 0082: 201, Dúchas © National Folklore Collection, UCD (translation from Irish): https://www.duchas.ie/en/cbes/4602708/4597353/4631117 (accessed December 2021).
28. Arnold van Gennep, The Rites of Passage (Chicago: University of Chicago

Press, 1972); Victor Turner, The Ritual Process: Structure and Anti-Structure (Ithaca: Cornell University Press, 1977).
29. IFC 903: 231-4.
30. Ó Catháin, The Festival of Brigit p.15.
31. IFC 903: 133-4.
32. Ó Catháin, The Festival of Brigit p.22.
33. IFC 902: 32.
34. See Lawrence Taylor, Occasions of Faith: An Anthropology of Irish Catholics (Dublin: Lilliput Press, 1995).
35. Charles O'Conor, Columbanus ad Hibernos, I: Or, A Letter from Columban to his Friend in Ireland (London: Payne, 1810) p.83.
36. IFC 694: 189 (translated from Irish).

Circles and a Square: Magical protection at the Maison Forte de Reignac, a fortified dwelling in the Dordogne region of France

Linda Wilson

History

The Maison Forte de Reignac is a fortified dwelling in the Vézère valley in the heart of the Dordogne region of France. The area is best known for its wealth of prehistoric sites including the painted cave of Lascaux, but there are also many castles and other fortified dwellings such as Commarque, Sauveboeuf, and Jumeillac. Many of these contain markings of interest to researchers into more recent history, but few have the abundance of riches found in the Maison Forte de Reignac.

The area is also noted for its limestone cliffs formed by the action of river water cutting down through the rock, deepening the valley sides and leaving behind deep natural terraces that have always lent themselves to human occupation. These cliffs saw their first phase of use in the Upper Palaeolithic and one site, Roc de Cazelle in the nearby Beaune valley, remained in use as late as 1966.

Fig. 1. Maison Forte de Reignac.

Excavations at Reignac revealed it was in use around 15000 BC. The wide ledges provided easily defensible shelters with an impressive view over the game-rich valley below, a nearby source of food, as the river was an easy supply of water for both animals and their hunters. The site was subsequently occupied in the Neolithic, the Bronze Age, and on into the Iron Age, as people followed the example of their predecessors and made use of this natural fortress in the cliff face. By 1000 AD it is likely that timber frames would have supported wattle and daub walls, making the inside areas warmer and more weather-proof. The site is believed to have remained in occupation throughout the turbulent medieval period and at some point its timbered exterior was replaced by stone, with narrow arrow-slit windows in the outer wall making the site even more formidably defensible.[1] Little historical information survives for Reignac's history during the Medieval period, but the fortified dwelling would have provided an important refuge in the many wars that ravaged the region.

The late 15th to early 16th century was a more stable period for the fortified house and its inhabitants, and the exterior is believed to have taken on the softer and more domestic aspect that can be seen today, with new window openings made in the façade. A capstone on an archway into the terraced area at the front of the house carries the date of 1667, indicating when that area was landscaped. It bears the inscription INMOTA MANEBIT, 'it will remain unchanged'.[2]

The only early illustration assigned to Reignac is a sketch by Sabine Baring-Gould.[3] However, there are significant differences between his published sketch and the house that can be seen today. The caption states: 'Chateau de Rignac. A renaissance château on the Vézère, built partly into and partly out of the overhanging cliff. Since the sketch was made a portion of the first archway has fallen'. This was presumed by Roussot and Roussout-Laroque to relate to Reignac, despite the difference in spelling.[4] There are places in the area with the name Rignac, but none could, by any stretch of the imagination, be described as 'on the Vézère'. If the sketch does relate to Reignac, it is problematic that it shows only two lines of windows at the front of the house, as well as other differences from the building as it now is. Baring-Gould's diaries show that he was in the area in 1882, although he is also known to have travelled in France with his parents in his youth.[5] As he is generally thought to have been an accurate sketch artist, substantial differences of this nature are surprising.[6] It is by no means certain that this sketch has been correctly captioned, and it should be treated with caution.

The Maison Forte de Reignac, a listed building since 1964, is now owned by archaeologist, prehistorian and historian Jean-Max Touron, whose passion for the past has led to him acquiring an extensive portfolio of sites in the Dordogne and the Lot, all restored and maintained to the highest standard. Reignac is open to visitors throughout the year. M. Touron's cooperation for this research has been invaluable. With his kind permission, a survey of the graffiti and protection marks was undertaken, and a full report is in progress.

Fig. 2. 'Chateau de Rignac', ?1882.

Although some hundred marks of various types were recorded, this paper will concentrate on the ones made to provide magical protection for the house and its inhabitants.

The Marks

The starting point for this study is inside the house, a date inscribed in a bay beside a window on the ground floor. In the stone at the bottom righthand corner of the window opening, a date of 1508 has been deeply carved, set in an oblong cartouche topped by two *fleurs de lys* at the corners. Roussot and Roussout-Laroque suggest this date is contemporaneous with the phase of remodelling that gave the house much of its current appearance.[7]

Very close to the date graffito, just above and to the left, is an impressive, interlinked compass-drawn design generally known in France as a *rosace*, 'rose-like': what in Britain would be called a daisy-wheel or multifoil. The marks in Reignac, and elsewhere, are best seen by raking light, which enhances the shadows of the lightly inscribed circles and petals, easily overlooked in strong sunlight. Luckily, this large multiple *rosace* design narrowly escaped damage from the fitting of both a timeline interpretation board and the Perspex protection given to the date itself, but that is probably more by accident than design, as marks like this are often overlooked, even by the most sympathetic of restorers. Sometimes they are simply not noticed, as is likely to have been the case here, and on other occasions they have been dismissed as unimportant and undeserving of further study. In a classic example of accidental damage, a large, beautiful daisy-wheel in the entrance gateway to Berkeley Castle in Gloucestershire was marred by a bright red box, part of the fire alarm system that could just as easily have been situated a few inches to the side.

Fig. 3. 1508 date.

Fig. 4. Rosace design adjacent to 1508 date.

Although designs such as this are commonly said to be 'compass-drawn',

59

and many will have been made this way, others were possibly made with implements such as shears, although with these it is difficult to keep the same diameter.[8] At its simplest, a piece of wood with two nails driven through it could be used. Here, the term compass-drawn and the French word *rosace* are used. Compass-drawn circles such as the *rosace* are one of the most common symbols found in the search for historic marks. They are also one of the most common types of apotropaic mark – incisions made with the intention of warding away evil. The *rosace* has ancient origins, but it is hard to say whether there is any direct connection between the designs found on classical Roman buildings and those that appear later in medieval church architecture. They also appear in a more informal way, possibly as a means of protection and maybe also a way of attracting good luck.[9]

When considering such beliefs, it should be kept in mind that people in the Middle Ages and even down to the early modern times lived in a world where evil could take many forms, with malign spirits entering a building through openings like doors, windows and chimneys. It is these openings that are most suggestive of a magical context at Reignac.

In the next chamber, known as the Great Room, there is a series of four interlocking circles on the righthand side of the window. A piece of ironwork to hang pans over a stone sink has been fixed to the wall inside the most complete of the circles. The circle is one of the simplest symbols and in many cultures represents the divine, the cosmos and eternity.[10] Simple compass-drawn circles of this type are familiar to anyone interested in marks on old buildings and are found as often in France as in Britain, on both stone and wood, in castles, churches and houses. On the left-hand side of this window, a large partial *rosace* is obscured by an interpretation panel, showing again how this sort of marking has become invisible to those working on the fabric of buildings.

Fig. 5. Interlocking circles.

Moving upwards, at the top of the staircase leading to the first floor there is a large double concentric circle, about 16 cm in diameter. Almost opposite is a smaller single compass-drawn circle in the outer side of the doorway of the room known as the *dortoir* (dormitory), believed to have been used as a common room and sleeping quarters for the servants. The doorways at either end of this room contain large W marks of the type often referred to as a

Fig. 6. (above left) Rosace partially obscured by interpretation panel.
Fig. 7. (above right) Concentric circles.

conjoined V or Marian mark. I am not aware of any other examples of this mark in the region, although it is amongst the most common marks found in Britain, and is widely known across Europe.[11]

This W or VV is the most controversial mark in our field of study. Timothy Easton proposed that it stands for *Virgo Virginum*, 'virgin of virgins', and invoked the protection of the Virgin Mary.[12] Others, however, think it represents nothing more than the initial W. If Easton's explanation is true, this mark can only have survived in England by being so deeply engrained in the popular psyche that it sailed unscathed through the Reformation, probably divorced from its original meaning along the way.

In many cases a W is clearly nothing more than an initial – it is always

Fig. 8. (above left) W in lefthand edge of doorway to the dortoir.
Fig. 9. (above right) W in righthand edge of doorway to the dortoir.

necessary to look closely at the context before attempting to categorise one as apotropaic. First, there may be another letter in close association with the first one in the same style etc. If so, the mark is likely to be nothing more than an initial. Secondly, the letter or letters may be close to a date. In such cases, they are probably nothing more than someone recording their presence at that moment in time. Thirdly, the mark may somewhere thought to need some form of magical protection. Here, keep in mind the phrase beloved of estate agents: 'location, location, location'.

In the case of the W marks at Reignac, they are each in the entrance to a room, possibly one for working-class occupants of the building. There are no other initials associated with these large and obvious marks, nor is there any date nearby. They are in doorways at either end of the room, a situation that calls for protective markings to guard against entry by malign forces.

These marks are at heights of 127 cm and 98 cm from floor level. Their protection seems focussed on doorways rather than the windows, as if the markings were made before windows were put in. In the sketch by Baring-Gould, these windows are missing; further research may establish whether these were added after the sketch was made, which seems unlikely, or whether the sketch has assigned to the wrong location, as is more probable.

The small antechamber at the end of the *dortoir* contains a large faint circle by one of the windows, and opposite this, an oblong motif with double crossed lines. Climbing to the second floor from here, it is possible to see the profile of the cliff from this section of the plan. The drawing room, at 60 square metres, is the largest room in the house. Here, in 2015, an impressive discovery was made when a section of plaster fell off the wall revealing a very rare example of enigmatic word puzzle – a SATOR square.

These squares are amongst the most enigmatic forms of magical protection.[13] Their meaning remains obscure and there are numerous radically different views on their meaning and origin. Of the earliest examples, two have been found in Pompeii. Some have proposed a pre-Christian religious origin in Mithraism; others look to Judaism, pointing to the use of alphabetic acrostics in Jewish exorcism. France contains several such squares, as does Britain. SATOR squares can take two forms, either arranged as SATOR and or as ROTAS. There are two Roman examples in England, one on

Fig. 10. SATOR square.

display in the Corinium museum in Cirencester and the other in Manchester Museum. Other examples can be found in the church at Alphamstone in Essex and in the churchyard in Rivington in Lancashire. The age of this stone is not known but it is believed to have come from a nearby private chapel in Anderton.

One of the most common explanations for these word squares is that the letters can be rearranged into two interlocking words PATERNOSTER, 'Our Father', with two As and Os left over; these are usually interpreted as Alpha and Omega.[14] However, William Baines casts doubt on this. He asserts that there 88 possible word squares that can be made up of five-letter Latin words, and demonstrates how different pseudo-Christian formulae can be abstracted from them, which this casts doubt on the Paternoster theory.[15] There is still no consensus on the square's meaning and if its devisors intended to keep a secret, they have certainly succeeded.

Interpretation of the example in Reignac depends on how these squares were regarded in the Middle Ages, for which Aymar Alphonse has found evidence from the area around Aurillac in the Haute-Auvergne region, about 136 km due east of Reignac.[16] This paper describes a fifteenth-century medical amulet kept in a small bag said to have been owned by the *'famille R...'* that was discreetly lent to women in childbirth to aid their labour. Amongst the many items in the bag was a bundle of documents including four manuscripts on vellum. At the bottom of one of these is a SATOR square surrounded by Latin text: *Hanc figuram mo[n]stra mulierem in partu et peperit*, 'show this figure to a woman giving birth and she will be delivered'.[17] The position of the square at the Maison Forte de Reignac, like that of the 1508 date graffito, suggests a magical use and protective function, perhaps as a charm to prevent malign influences entering the dwelling through the new openings in its once-forbidding exterior, perhaps to confer some medical protection on

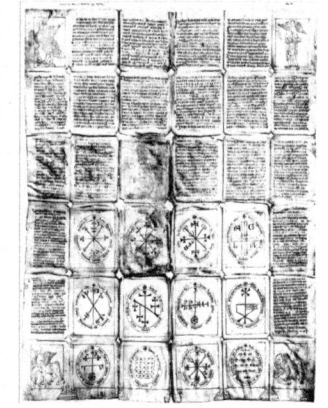

Fig. 11. The Aurillac manuscript; SATOR square third from left on bottom row.

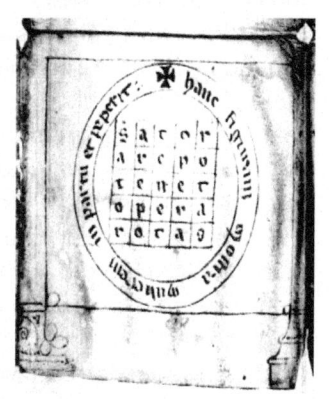

Fig. 12. Relevant section of Fig. 11. enlarged.

the women of the house, perhaps both.

A climb to the upper terraces of Reignac offers a commanding view up and down the valley and makes it easy to understand why this site continued in use for both habitation and defence over many millennia. Much old plaster remains intact on the walls of the upper level. Here, the greatest concentration of graffiti left behind by visitors to Reignac can be found on both the plaster and the exposed stonework on the walls of a small room said to have been used by the alchemist Léopold de Bonaventure, who is said to have lived in the Maison Forte in 1386 experimenting on the transmutation of base metals into gold, and actually succeeding with an elixir of immortality as well as a panacea for all ills – but the truth of that story is anyone's guess.[18] The age of these structures is unknown, as there isn't any written history of Reignac and no records have survived.

Amidst the names, dates, and other graffiti on one wall are three large, very deeply cut compass-drawn circles each with a large obvious central point. On the left-hand side of the Alchemist's Room, the plaster is fragmentary in places, but it is possible to see the remains of a large set of concentric circles. Close by is another circle, a pair of concentric circles and something that resembles a spider's web design. On this, and every other wall of this building, is a plethora of riches for the historic graffiti hunter, testifying to the fact that Reignac was a popular place for visitors throughout the nineteenth and twentieth centuries.

Visitors leaving the Maison Forte today might spot a curious collection of symbols inscribed on obviously modern stone on the recently reconstructed wall at the top of the steps at the side of the building. These comprise a very neat rosace, an eight-pointed star, an IHS and a shield. These are said to have been made by Alain Roussot, co-author of the short paper on the 1508 date.[19] Unfortunately, M. Roussot died in 2013, before I began my research on Reignac and its enigmatic marks, so it was impossible to ask him why he chose to adorn the exit from the house in this way. Jean-Max Touron believes these represent the marks that the inhabitants of the Maison Forte would have known. The reason for the rosace is obvious as the ones next to the 1508 date could hardly have been missed when that was studied, and they are extremely common in the area. The IHS is equally obvious as that is a well-known Christogram, and in Reignac there is one on the iron door of an old bread oven.

The eight-pointed star, sometimes known as an auseklis cross, was more of a puzzle: though it is common in the region, there are no marks of this type in the house. Eventually the likely reason for its inclusion was found, hiding in plain sight in the fireplace at the back of the chimney in the main room. The fire-back is not original to the house but fits the sixteenth-century setting, and the eight-pointed star is often found on fire-backs in the region; there is one in the castle of Jumeillac. The design also features in alchemy. This particular mark provides a cautionary tale, as Champion refers to an eight-pointed star in Reignac, without knowing that this was, in fact, a very modern addition.[20] The error is believed to have occurred as only a photograph of the mark was supplied to the author.[21]

This set of modern marks illustrates how quickly information about the intention and even the identity of mark makers can be lost; in just this way the original Christian symbolism of designs was lost, as marks transitioned into folk belief and protective charms.

At this stage in the search for marks, no check had been made on the exterior of the building – which would have been a failure in due diligence, since a search of the front wall almost immediately revealed more circles. This came as no surprise as it was obvious by then that the inhabitants of Reignac had a special fondness for positioning circles beside windows. Those on the exterior are extremely weathered but can still be made out. Two sets of concentric circles appear on the same block immediately outside the ground floor windows. The moral of this story is that when conducting a survey, always check the exterior as well as the interior.

Conclusion

The inhabitants of Reignac inscribed numerous protective signs and symbols into the fabric of the building. They are of a type seen elsewhere throughout Europe in contexts that make it clear they were intended to provide magical protection to supplement its defensive position and the strength of its walls.

These markings include several compass-drawn multifoils, concentric circles and single compass-drawn circles as well as the debated W mark and the even more enigmatic and enduringly fascinating SATOR square. The position of the main markings is

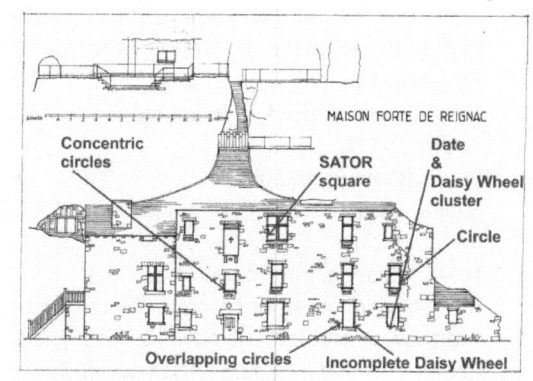

Fig. 13. Position of marks shown on architect's drawing of Reignac.

indicated on an architect's drawing of the building.

The Maison Forte de Reignac is an example of how the addition of magical defences may have brought a measure of comfort and additional protection to the inhabitants of the building, at a time when the old frontal defences may have seemed weakened by the formation of new window openings in the outer wall of a once formidable fortress.

Acknowledgements

Photographs are by Anthea Hawdon (3, 4, 7, and 8), Graham Mullan (1 and 10) and myself (5, 6 and 9). The architect's drawing in fig. 13 is used with permission of Jean-Max Touron. Fig. 2 is from Baring-Gould, *Cliff Castles*, and fig. 11 from Alphonse, 'Le sachet accoucheur'.

I am extremely grateful to the following for all their help and support with this research: Jean-Max Touron for such generous access to the Maison Forte on numerous occasions and for allowing me to conduct the survey of the marks; Graham Mullan for accompanying me on many photographic trips; Anthea Hawdon for her invaluable help with the survey; Claude Lacombe and Rebecca Ireland for help with research; Martin Graebe for his insights into the work of Sabine Baring-Gould; Kati Barr-Taylor for help with the translation of the original research proposal that led to this work and last but by no means least, Brian Hoggard, Jeremy Harte and John Billingsley of Hidden Charms for the opportunity to present this work at the third Hidden Charms symposium in Chester.

Notes

1. Titia Carrizey-Jasick and Jean-Max Touron, *Maison Forte de Reignac* (Sarlat: M.C.D Imprimeurs, 2009).
2. Alain Roussot and Julia Roussot-Larroque, 'Inscriptions datées à Reignac, Commune de Tursac', *Bulletin de la Société Historique et Archéologique du Périgord*, 103 (1975) pp.131–2.
3. Sabine Baring-Gould, *Cliff Castles and Cave Dwellings of Europe* (London: Seeley 1911).
4. Roussot and Roussout-Laroque, 'Inscriptions datées à Reignac'.
5. Sabine Baring-Gould, *Further Reminiscences 1864–1894* (London: Bodley Head, 1925).
6. Martin Graebe, pers. comm.
7. Roussot and Roussout-Laroque, 'Inscriptions datées à Reignac'.
8. Matthew Champion, *Medieval Graffiti: The Lost Voices of England's Churches* (London: Ebury, 2015) pp.38–9.
9. Matthew Champion, 'Magic on the walls: ritual protection marks in the medieval church' in *Physical Evidence for Ritual Acts, Sorcery and Witchcraft*

in *Christian Britain: A Feeling for Magic* ed. Ronald Hutton (Basingstoke: Palgrave Macmillan, 2016) pp.19-28; Timothy Easton, 'Apotropaic symbols and other measures for protecting buildings against misfortune' in *Physical Evidence* ed. Ronald Hutton pp.44-50.
10. Heather Child and Dorothy Colles, *Christian Symbols Ancient and Modern: A Handbook for Students* (London: G. Bell and Sons, 1971) p.27.
11. Champion, 'Magic on the walls' pp.19, 29-30; Matthew Champion, 'Le langage secret des graffitis' in *Sur Les Murs* ed. Laure Pressac (Paris: Editions du Patrimoine, Centres des Monuments Nationaux, 2018) p.102.
12. Easton, 'Apotropaic symbols' pp.42-3.
13. Duncan Fishwick, 'On the origin of the Rotas-Sator square', *Harvard Theological Review* 57 (1964) pp. 39-53.
14. J. Gwyn Griffith, '"Arepo" in the magic "Sator" square', *Classical Review* 21 (1971) pp.6-8.
15. William Baines, 'The Rotas-Sator square', *New Testament Studies* 33 (1987) pp. 469-76.
16. Aymar Alphonse, 'Contribution à l'étude du folklore de la Haute-Auvergne. Le sachet accoucheur et ses mystères', *Annales du Midi* 38 (1926) pp.346-7, plate IV.
17. Monica Green, *The Trotula: An English Translation of the Medieval Compendium of Women's Medicine* (Philadelphia PA: University of Pennsylvania Press, 2002).
18. Carrizey-Jasick and Touron, *Maison Forte de Reignac*.
19. Jean-Max Touron, pers. comm.
20. Champion, 'Le langage secret des graffitis'.
21. Matthew Champion, pers. comm.

X Marks the Post: The use of the X as an apotropaic symbol

Chris Wood

Many marks and signs are traditionally used to protect or bless objects, buildings, people and animals. However, their use can also be purely decorative. One of the simplest, and therefore perhaps most debateable, is the group of marks based on the X.

X marks are frequent on many types of antique object, but especially wrought-iron door furniture, bone scoops and the so-called 'witch posts' found in some seventeenth-century houses in, predominantly, Yorkshire. They may be straightforward or elongated Xs, or strings of Xs; they can be Xs flanked by two uprights, or with horizontal lines above and below. They may be related to more extensive cross-hatching, lattice or diaper work, to patterns in brickwork, Romanesque stone carving, or even Irish interlace, but there is something distinctive about the examples found singly or accompanied only by short lines, especially as these are often found in significant places in need of protection, such as points of entry into a house, or marked prominently on an object used for a task which could be harmed by malefic influence. However, the meaning and magical intent may well be different in different contexts.

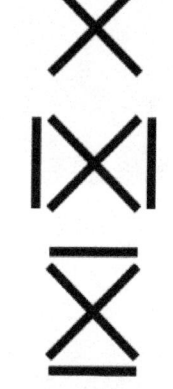

Fig. 1. Examples of X marks.

X marks occur in other contexts too, carved in stone or scratched on furniture. Whether these have meanings similar to the marks in metalwork, bone and heck posts will have to be the subject of further work. Furthermore, traditions vary. The focus here is primarily on the English context. As Marc Robben (this volume) points out, whilst there are common threads, significant differences in architectural practice and meaning separate England from the Continent, and these were in place well before the rupture of the Reformation. Likewise, diaspora communities such as those in North America have developed internally and interacted with indigenous traditions to create new expressions.[1]

Wrought ironwork

X marks appear frequently on antique metalwork in significant locations, especially latches, clasps, locks and hinges. Occasionally there is a punch mark in each of the angles. Wall anchors are often in the form of an X as well; on the continent, these are seen as protection against lightning, but X marks

69

stamped on wall anchors are more common on the continent too.²

Some of the best preserved older examples are to be found in medieval churches, where they appear on latches, locks and lock-straps, securing doors, windows and parish chests. Many of these are Victorian and later

Fig. 2. (top left) Early seventeenth-century latch on the front door of the Tudor House Museum, Southampton.
Fig. 3. (top right) Victorian latch in the church of St John Maddermarket, Norwich.
Fig. 4. (bottom left) Wall anchor on the church of St Helen, Norwich.
Fig. 5. (bottom right) X-shaped wall anchor, Brasenose Lane, Oxford.

reproductions, but some are much older. Jane Geddes illustrates English examples of the |X| mark from the fifteenth century, single Xs from the fourteenth, and X or lozenge marks along straps from the twelfth.³ According to Linda Hall, the mark went out of fashion in the course of the eighteenth century, before its Victorian revival.⁴

Timothy Easton relates that in 1992 a Suffolk blacksmith told him that the |X| represents the barring of entry between the door or window jambs. Although it seems plausible, this evidence from the late twentieth century could be a modern rationalisation as much as an articulation of traditional understanding.⁵ Other blacksmiths see it as a traditional decoration only.

Many X marks from the Victorian era may be decorative but others, especially in churches, are found at key points of entry, such as doors, churchyard gates and even gates in the altar rail. Such places are also often marked with upright crosses. All of this suggests that the X may also be a means of marking the place as Christ's property.

Older Metalwork
Archaeology presents earlier examples, such as late medieval bronze purse bars (probably representing binding), iron pins, bracelets from Viking silver hoards, and Anglo-Saxon bronze strap ends.[6]

Fig. 6. (above left) Hinge of a churchyard gate, church of St Margaret of Antioch, Cley-next-the-Sea, Norfolk.

Fig. 7. (above right) Door furniture, church of St Michael and All Angels, Ledbury, Herefordshire.

Tantalisingly, very similar marks appear on some Iron Age bronze metalwork, such as keys.[7] The Landesmuseum Württemberg in Stuttgart has a linch pin marked on one end with a double X and transverse lines above and between the Xs. The opposite end has a representation of a human head and arms, which may have been apotropaic.[8] One could speculate that the X was doubled to afford additional protection to the vulnerable nether regions of the apotropaic human!

Heck Posts ('Witch Posts')
A heck, spere or speer is a partition in a timber-framed building. It is a feature of many cottages, farmhouses and inns built in the seventeenth century and provided with a passage across the building to link front and back doors. Two rooms lead off this passage, and the hearth in the main room is protected from draughts by a short heck, ending in a stout post supporting a cross-beam or bressummer, which in turn holds up the smoke hood of an inglenook fireplace. The heck post has often been carved or given functional additions.[9]

Some 20 of these heck posts have a prominent

Fig. 8. Bronze linch pin from Grabenstetten, Germany, second–first century BC, length 111mm (Landesmuseum Württemberg (Stuttgart) A 32/17).

Fig. 9. (right) An impression of a heck post in situ, based on that in Stang End, Danby (Ryedale Folk Museum, Hutton-le-Hole).

X near the top, often with a series of rounded lines or billets horizontally across the post underneath. They are associated with buildings on the North York Moors (with a further two in Lancashire), and date from the mid-seventeenth century. Whilst they are generally known today as 'witch posts', this name was not used until the end of the nineteenth century.[10]

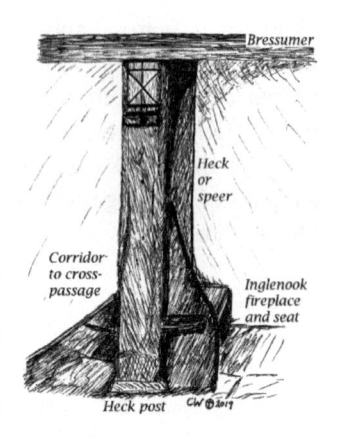

Joseph Ford relates the folk memory that these X marks were carved by a priest at the end of a ritual called 'laying the witch', to counteract malefic witchcraft affecting the farm:

> After this mysterious ceremony was over and the power of the witch was supposed to have been rendered nil, it was the custom of the Priest to cut the Roman figure X on the upright oak post which went up to the low ceiling. ... This mark cut in the post by the Priest meant that the Witch's spell could not operate for evil any further into the dwelling or beyond the post.[11]

This description raises three issues. First, because the 'witch post' stood at the notional centre of the house, it faced away from the passage by the heck partition, and would still have allowed any malign influence down the chimney to operate throughout the inglenook. Second, these posts are recorded without reference to witchcraft as late as the donation of examples to Oxford's Pitt Rivers Museum in 1870 and 1893 by Canon J.C. Atkinson (also of Danby parish), although in 1892 he does refer to one as an 'assumed' witch post, suggesting some currency by then.[12] Third, the grooves on most posts are very deeply cut with carpenters' tools, which seems unlikely for an operation carried out by a priest at the end of a ceremony. In several examples, the section with the X and billets stands proud of the surface of the post because a thicker section has been carefully worked, or in some examples a section below has been cut away, and this could not have been the culmination of a priest's rite and may well have been done before the post was installed.

However, the stated involvement of a priest is revealing. The late Peter Walker, writing as Nicholas Rhea, argued that if a *priest* was involved in the seventeenth century, then it was almost certainly a *Catholic* priest, and one who was practising his faith in times of persecution at that. Rhea researched one such priest, Father Nicholas Postgate, who walked around the Moors performing illicit masses in farmhouses from 1662 until he was arrested and executed in 1679. Rhea considered Ford's 'mysterious ceremony' to have been a blessing on the house that was to serve as a secret church, with the X mark functioning as a sign that it was thenceforth a Catholic 'safe house'.[13] The X makes much more sense as the mark of a house blessing than as an apotropaic defensive device, especially as it had powerful religious meanings itself.

Father Postgate was apparently devoted to the Five Wounds of Christ, a symbol used extensively in Catholic resistance to Protestantism. It is based on the wounds to the hands and feet of Jesus, at the four corners, and the wound in his side, transferred to his heart, in the centre. This could, perhaps, be reduced to an X.[14] Alternatively, the X could simply be the symbol of Christ, being the first letter of his name in Greek, used even today as an abbreviation in Xtian and Xmas. Whatever the meaning, if the mark was originated by Postgate, or used by him and a few others, it might explain why it is so localised.

However, whilst X-marked heck posts are only known from one small area of Britain, something similar is to be found across the North Sea in the eastern Netherlands and the German border districts. In this region it is used on the outside and so functions more clearly as a mark of protection, at a key point of entry and of a supporting structure. In these areas, there is a tradition of marking an X on the central post (*stiepel*) against which the double doors of a barn close. The earliest known form, from the seventeenth and eighteenth centuries, is the simple X, with or without horizontal bars above and below, carved as part of the post's manufacture. These marks developed over time, with the horizontal bars becoming attached to the top and bottom of a stretched X in what has become known as an hourglass motif. Other symbols, such as lozenges, hearts, upright crosses, chalices and daisy wheels also appear, often painted rather than carved. Significantly, these *stiepeltekens* are from predominantly Catholic districts.[15] Rhea suggested a link to Douai University, where Father Postgate studied from 1621 to 1630, and which was in the Spanish Netherlands until 1714.[16]

Christian Pillars?
A post or pillar with a Christian symbol at the top is common in the form of Celtic and Anglo-Scandinavian high crosses, slab crosses and similar structures. These have been shown to represent Christ as the Tree of Life and

the paradisal source of the waters of life, in a quite visceral way, especially when rain water alters the appearance of the stone.[17] Such interpretations may help explain why the Cross itself was seen as idolatrous by many Protestants in the Reformation.[18]

Some of these monuments have narrow crosses, barely wider than the post, and the X-marked heck post may have appeared similar. Whether or not the X represented the Five Wounds of Christ, or the first letter of Christ's name, it could also have portrayed the Cross itself, and by extension Christ in Paradise, dispensing blessing on the home. The post becomes a cross, which becomes the Cross, and the house becomes Paradise.

The X-shaped cross is found as a Christian symbol, most commonly associated with St Andrew. This was a late development, probably in twelfth-century Britain: it may have been a conflation of the *Chi Rho* monogram and Scottish kings' devotion to the saint, or it could have been a misinterpretation of images of the saint crucified on a tree with forking branches.[19]

However, an X carved into a surface can be seen in two ways: as the X itself, but also as the shape left standing in relief around it: an equal-armed cross with triangular arms (Fig. 11, top left).[20]

There is an interesting folkloric link between X-marked heck posts and one Yorkshire high cross. There is a tradition of hiding a crooked sixpence in a hole in the 'witch post', and a knitting needle in a groove at the top. When the butter would not turn, which was assumed to be because of witchcraft, the knitting needle was used to remove the sixpence from the hole and the coin was put in the churn, so countering the curse.[21]

A similar custom is recorded by Joseph Ford at (Young) Ralph's Cross, which stands roughly at the centre of the North York Moors, near the head of Rosedale, and is now the emblem of the North York Moors National Park. The story goes that a farmer by the name of Ralph found the body of a penniless traveller, dead from exposure, and was so moved that he had a stone cross erected on the spot to indicate that shelter was within reach at an inn just a few miles away. He had the head of the cross carved with a hollow so that passers-by might deposit coins, which other penniless wayfarers might use.[22] The story is unlikely, particularly as the cross stands nine feet tall, but the placing of coins in a cross-marked pillar, for use in need, is resonant![23] It also recalls the Anglo-Saxon cures which required moss or lichen that had grown on stone or wooden crosses.[24]

Whatever the original purpose of these X-marked posts, knowledge of the custom seems to have declined in the eighteenth century. Towards the end of that century heck posts were often removed in rebuilding work to be reused as lintels in out-buildings, where a number of the preserved examples were found.[25]

Bone Scoops or Apple Corers

Scoops carved from the metapodial (lower leg) bones of sheep served several purposes: removing the cores from apples, sampling cheeses, providing eating utensils for those who had lost their teeth, and acting as love tokens cut, carved and given by young men to their sweethearts in the same way as Welsh Love Spoons.[26] In all probability, they served many purposes and were cut and carved accordingly. Analysis of staining and wear marks would clarify actual use, but this has seldom been done; where it has, the implications are significant. Similar tools found on London's Thames foreshore turned out to be fids for rope working.[27]

The standard of decoration varies tremendously, with some ornate examples rivalling Love Spoons, while others are relatively crude, presumably work-a-day tools. A very common feature, however, is the X, usually as |X|. The meaning generally ascribed to the mark is a wish for good luck.[28]

The earliest securely dated examples of bone scoops of this kind are from the seventeenth century, perhaps reflecting greater availability of the fine-toothed saws which could cut the bone.[29] This gives some context to the decoration. Whilst the folk craft of making bone scoops remained common into the twentieth century, some had been made for sale by French prisoners of war who were interned around Britain during the Napoleonic Wars (1797–1814) along with ornate bone and straw work.[30] However, the provenance of scoops found for sale is rarely secure and sellers frequently claim their items to be of PoW manufacture for marketing purposes.

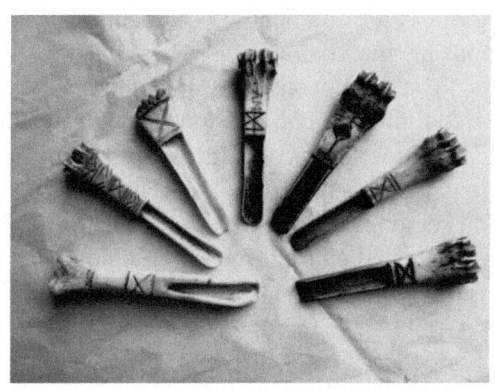

Fig.10. Bone scoops from the Ickeny Collection (EAMMM 2004.1, 2018.2, 2020.4.1 to 5).

What Does the X Mean?

As well as being purely decorative, X marks have a variety of purposes and meanings. In the modern world, the mark can mean both a positive choice (on a ballot slip) and a rejection and barring, as well as the place to click when closing a computer file, an abbreviation for 'ex...', and a symbol of something unknown. The categories below overlap too: the same thing can, at one and the same time, be decorative, practical, symbolic, devotional and protective!

Practical
There are practical reasons for using an X mark or lattice. It can give a better grip, and so is useful on handles and anything else that has to be held, such as bone scoops and fids. The X shape also gives structural strength when it holds the legs of a table together.

Stonemasons and carpenters use various marks to ensure their materials are cut, shaped and assembled correctly. One of these is what has become known as the 'butterfly cross', which looks like a stretched *dagaz* rune as discussed below, but is used to align the work to plumb lines and levels.[31]

Craftspeople also have identifying marks, although the X and its derivatives are too abundant and simple to do this well. On the other hand, the X is a traditional way of signing for those who cannot write, a way of making one's mark.

The X is a precise way of identifying a spot, whether on a treasure map or a 'spot the ball' competition. It is also an efficient way of covering a space and can be seen in such crafts as cross stitch, basketry, thatching and metalwork (e.g. lattice screens). It is used in this way in decoration, such as diaper work on ceramics, and illustration, in the form of cross-hatching. When cut deep it provides an efficient means of drainage, as on the stone fruit presses still to be found in some parts of the countryside.[32]

Symbolic
Perhaps the X's most obvious meaning, apart from negation, is as the sign of a kiss, a token of love and affection. This is connected to its sense of a gift or exchange, in turn linked to the *gyfu* rune. It can be symbolic of skill as well. Craftspeople will add decoration to a piece of work simply because they can. Leaving a blank space would look less skilled, less professional. The X also stands directly for the number 10, as the Roman numeral, which is the origin of the Latin adjective for the X-shaped cross, *decussata*.

Similar marks can also represent bindings: generally double lines or bands forming crosses or simply at an angle across a surface. Medieval purse bars and Anglo-Saxon and Viking-era bone and antler combs frequently have them.[33] Neolithic chalk cylinders appear to be simulacra of rope-wound drums for measuring.[34] Late medieval church monuments sometimes feature swaddled babies, known as 'chrysoms', and these have criss-cross banding.[35] The *fasces*, ceremonial regalia of high magistrates in ancient Rome and a symbol of political and legal power in modern times, was a bundle of rods tied tightly together round an axe as restrained powers of punishment.[36] Binding with cords or straps is the common element here, with symbolic and potentially magical binding power.[37]

Politically, the X is most common as the Scottish saltire or cross of St Andrew, and stands for Scottish identity. It also appears in heraldry, which provides the saltires on some municipal flags in Brabant. Others derive from the Burgundy Cross, as do Spanish military flags, as this was the flag of the Spanish Netherlands adopted from the Duke of Burgundy, whose emblem honoured St Andrew, although it also resembles a Carolingian crossed-branch motif.[38] The Irish saltire of St Patrick is a modern concoction by the Order of St Patrick, established in 1782.[39]

Religious
The religious connotations of marks on objects in Western Europe are predominantly Christian. The Cross is the central image of Christianity, but usually the upright, Latin cross, or various equal-armed crosses. The X-shaped cross *decussata* is uncommon, save as the cross of St Andrew.[40]

The first letter of Christ in Greek is the X (*Chi*) and can indicate the whole name, as can the first *two* letters, as the Chi Rho monogram used by the Emperor Constantine as a battle standard. A further Greek monogram is that of St Michael (Fig. 11, top middle), also found in simplified forms, and a well-attested protective mark.[41]

Lattice work survives in the ironwork of some medieval church doors and Jane Geddes interprets it as representing the fence or gate that shut off Eden. For Christians, this Paradise is regained in Christ's Cross and, by extension, in the Church which lies behind the doors decorated with the lattice.[42] More generally, the X marks on church ironwork seem to be placed both to keep out evil by the sign of Christ, and to mark the space within as Christ's.

Although not necessarily appearing as an X, the Five Wounds of Christ form a *quincunx* pattern (see below), which appears to have been used as a symbol of Catholic sympathies following the Reformation, appearing subtly above the doors of well-to-do recusant homes such as Benthall Hall in Shropshire.[43] This may also be the origin of the line 'Five for the symbols at your door' in the traditional song *Green Grow the Rushes, O!*[44]

Lastly, the X with a horizontal bar on the top and the bottom can also be seen as a pair of triangles with their points touching (Fig. 11, top right). These are the same triangles as conjoin in the Star of David, but separated out so that they just meet, the point of contact being the 'straight and narrow gate' between Earth and Heaven – Christ and the Church.[45]

Apotropaic

There are three basic, overlapping ways to protect someone or something magically, and the X mark can be used in all three:
1) direct opposition: blocking, repulsion, and anti-aggressive action such as binding and trapping;
2) deflection: turning aside the effect or attention, hiding and being 'invisible';
3) blessing: a boost to the magical immune system, an overwhelming, positive spiritual influence, or simply a good-luck charm.

The single |X| marks on bone scoops have generally been identified as wishes for good luck, whereas on metalwork they are seen as barring entry.[46] The 'butterfly crosses' (where not utilitarian construction marks) may bar entry, confound malefic attack in an endless knot, or perhaps invoke protection derived from the *dagaz* rune (see below) or a simplified version of the St Michael monogram.

It may well be that people also saw craftsmen's marks, on timber, stone and metal, as symbolic of the mysteries of a skilled craft, beyond the ken of the uninitiated, and therefore used them as protective marks. Done with intent and belief, there is no reason to suppose they would not be effective.

Just as the X is a practical way of covering a space in terms of craft or drawing, so it is in magic. Forming an X by carrying out an operation at the centre and at each of the four corners of a piece of land or a house (whether or not calling on the directional powers) seems to be a widespread technique, seen in Europe and in the African-American tradition of natural magic, Hoodoo. In the latter case it has been labelled '*quincunx* magic'.[47]

Magical and Cosmological

The *quincunx* is a pattern of five dots, as they appear on a die, which can be represented as an X and by extension a lozenge or lattice pattern. One of its foremost exponents was Sir Thomas Browne, who wrote a short book entirely on the subject.[48] The *quincunx*, along with its extension, the lattice or network, is an alchemical framework, symbolic of the formation of the material world, an illusion which we make real, just as the drawing technique of cross-hatching creates an illusion that effectively becomes real. Our intent to make something real is also indicated by putting our mark (X) on something. The lattice may indeed represent sin, the barrier to Paradise.[49] The world we create for ourselves separates us from God, from Paradise, or from the abyss of potentiality. Equally, a lattice or mesh can entrap malevolent entities, which explains the use of graffiti mesh marks.[50]

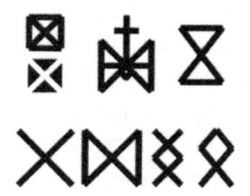

Fig. 11. Christian and runic symbols. Top row, left to right: two ways of seeing an incised X cross, the monogram of St Michael, and the straight and narrow way. Bottom row: four runes often thought to be present in angular markings: gyfu/gebo, dagaz, inguz and othala/odal.

Runes?

Angular marks are easily seen as Germanic runes. However, it is easier to carve straight lines than curves, so, for instance, an attempt to carve an infinity symbol is likely to resemble a *dagaz* rune. The runes often proposed as lying behind X marks and 'butterfly crosses' (as well as patterns in brickwork) are as follows, with a modern interpretation of their meanings, based on the rune poems (see also Fig. 11).

Gyfu/gebo	Gift, generosity, reciprocity, consecration
Dagaz	Day and night, sunlight, protection, invisibility[51]
Inguz	Prosperity, well-being, fertility, the hearth
Othala/odal	(Ancestral) home, prosperity, family

There must always be doubts about applying modern meanings to past usage, even when these are based on the rune poems. Meanings have changed. For instance, Stephen Mitchell analyses Norse charm inscriptions and shows that the rune *nauthiz* was once associated with the dead and ghosts, rather than the sense of need conveyed by the rune poems.[52] Evidence from early modern grimoires in Iceland, a country with a strong runic heritage, suggests that the letter-runes were by then a minor part of magic, that this usage was the preserve of a few, and that their shapes varied considerably.[53] This would not rule out folk-usage, but meanings would then be even less certain. Furthermore, even if X marks did derive ultimately from runes (and the Celtic bronze items mentioned above also militate against this) such an origin does not imply a *direct* link.

Certainly, the dating of bone scoops and heck posts would seem to rule out any direct link to runes, although both *gyfu* and *dagaz* may well lie in the background as the precursor to the use of the X as a symbol of a kiss (*gyfu*) and as the likely origin of German and Dutch shutter decoration (*dagaz*).[54]

One could speculate that Dutch *stiepelteken* may derive from *gyfu* and that they may derive from the same source as the Yorkshire carved heck posts, but that is not the same as saying that the heck posts were carved with this rune in mind, especially if Christian symbolism was intended.

However, magical practitioners use whatever resources they have available. The X mark has had and still has many meanings and uses worldwide. If one's magic draws upon a particular source, and the X mark connects with that source, then it is entirely appropriate to make, use and consecrate the mark with that understanding. However, if the mark in question was made by someone else, perhaps a long time ago, then we need to be aware that the maker and user may well have had very different things in mind. It is not that a form of magic or belief is 'right' or 'wrong', just that using one system with an object consecrated in another is counter-productive; like mixing languages, the effect is at best garbled.

Conclusion

People in the past would not necessarily have interpreted or used the X mark in the way that we do, and the mark could have had multiple interpretations and uses, not only in different contexts, but even in similar ones. It has always been thus, which is one reason the meanings of symbols change! My carpenter's mark may be your *dagaz* rune or someone else's simplified protective glyph of St Michael. Decoration can also be functional – practically, religiously or magically. We must not back-project our assumptions, nor use these assumptions to dismiss possibilities out of hand. What matters in magic is intent and the intent of people in the past cannot be assumed.

Having said that, it does seem that the X can indeed be a barring sign, but it can also be a blessing (whether or not invoking Christ), and the latter may be the more significant in many cases, especially churches.

Acknowledgements

All photographs and drawings are by myself except for Fig. 7, for which I am grateful to Brian Hoggard. Thanks to Nathan Stafford-King at the Tudor House Museum in Southampton for kindly supplying the history of the door (Fig. 2) in 2019.

Notes

1. See for instance Walter Richard Wheeler, 'Magical dwelling: apotropaic building practices in the New World Dutch cultural hearth', in *Hidden Charms 2: Exploring the Magical Protection of Buildings, Transactions of the Hidden Charms Conference 2018* ed. John Billingsley, Jeremy Harte and

Brian Hoggard (Hebden Bridge: Northern Earth, 2019) pp.86–115.
2. Marc Robben, pers. comm.
3. Jane Geddes, *Medieval Decorative Ironwork in England* (London: Society of Antiquaries, 1999).
4. Linda Hall, *Period House Fixtures and Fittings 1300–1900* (Newbury: Countryside Books, 2005) p.60.
5. Timothy Easton, 'Ritual marks on historic timber', *Weald and Downland Open Air Museum Journal* (Spring 1999) pp.22–8; Timothy Easton, 'Ritual marks on historic timber', *3rd Stone* 38 (2000) pp.11–17; Timothy Easton, 'Apotropaic symbols and other measures for protecting buildings against misfortune', in *Physical Evidence for Ritual Acts, Sorcery and Witchcraft in Christian Britain: A Feeling for Magic* ed. Ronald Hutton (Basingstoke: Palgrave Macmillan, 2015) pp.39–67.
6. For purse bars, see Portable Antiquities Scheme (www.finds.org.uk) SUSS-295D53 and SUSS-C9EB44 (both from Sussex); Ashmolean AN1950.295, illustrated in Eleanor Standley, *Trinkets and Charms: The Use, Meaning and Significance of Dress Accessories 1300–1700* (Monograph 78, Oxford: Oxford University School of Archaeology, 2013) p.63; NM.257 in Nigel Mills, *Medieval Artefacts* (Witham: Greenlight, 2003) p.98. For iron pins, no. 1233, figure 101, in Dominic Tweddle, *The Archaeology of York, The Small Finds: Finds from Parliament Street and Other Sites in the City Centre* (London: Council for British Archaeology, 1986) pp.228–9. For Viking bracelets, James Graham-Campbell, *The Cuerdale Hoard and Related Viking-Age Silver and Gold from Britain and Ireland in the British Museum* (second edition, London: British Museum Press, 2013). For Anglo-Saxon strap ends, Portable Antiquities Scheme (www.finds.org.uk) NMS-6BB7DB (fifth-sixth century) and NMS-234024 (ninth century), both Norfolk, with AS36 and AS37 (ninth-tenth century), in Nigel Mills, *Anglo-Saxon & Viking Artefacts* (Witham: Greenlight, 2001) p.25.
7. E.g. figure 691 in Helmut Birkhan (tr. Sophie Kidd), *Celts: Images of their Culture* (Vienna: Verlag der Österreichischen Akademie der Wissenschaften, 1999) p.364; RB237 (first-second century) in Nigel Mills, *Celtic and Roman Artefacts* (Witham: Greenlight, 2000) p.80.
8. Figure 516 in Birkhan, *Celts* p.301; Landesmuseum Württemberg, 'Achsnagel', https://www.landesmuseum-stuttgart.de/sammlung/sammlung-online/dk-details/? dk_object_id=773 (accessed November 2021).
9. Ronald William Brunskill, *Timber Building in Britain* (second edition, London: Victor Gollancz, 1999); Ronald William Brunskill, *Traditional Buildings of Britain: An Introduction to Vernacular Architecture and its Revival* (third edition, London: Cassell, 2004); Raymond Harland Hayes and Joseph Gatt

Rutter, *Cruck-Framed Buildings in Ryedale & Eskdale* (Scarborough: Scarborough and District Archaeological Society, 1972).
10. Mary Nattrass, 'Witch posts and early dwellings in Cleveland', *Yorkshire Archaeological Journal* 39 (1956) pp.136–46; Nigel Pennick, *Earth Harmony: Places of Power, Holiness and Healing* (second edition, Chieveley: Capall Bann, 1997); Nigel Pennick, *Pagan Magic of the Northern Tradition: Customs, Rites, and Ceremonies* (Rochester VT: Destiny, 2015); Nicholas Rhea, *Blessed Nicholas Postgate: Martyr of the Moors* (Leominster: Gracewing, 2012) pp.99–113.
11. Joseph Ford, *Some Reminiscences and Folk Lore of Danby Parish and District* (Whitby: Horne & Son, 1953) pp.95–6.
12. Rhea, *Blessed Nicholas Postgate* p.107; Hayes and Rutter, *Cruck-framed Buildings*. Note also that, whilst 'witch posts' are supposedly made of rowan, all examples (except reproductions) are of oak, like the rest of the house timbers. One could perhaps also speculate that the similarity of 'heck' to 'hex' may have been a factor in the popularity of the naming.
13. Rhea, *Blessed Nicholas Postgate* pp.108–9. The distinction that Rhea makes between a 'priest' (Catholic) and a 'church priest' (C. of E.) leaves doubt, however, as Ford (*Some Reminiscences*, note 14) writes of a 'parish priest' in a way that suggests a C. of E. affiliation. On the other hand, he makes no mention of Catholicism in his book, where the religious division is between Anglicans and Methodists.
14. Rhea, *Blessed Nicholas Postgate* p.126.
15. Jan Jans and Everhard Jans, *Gevel- en Stiepeltekens in Oost-Nederland* (Enschede: van der Loeff, 1974). See also www.zweerink.nl/index.php/stiepeltekens (accessed November 2021).
16. Nicholas Rhea, 'Farewell to witchposts – hello to priest marks and *stiepelteken*', www.nicholasrhea.co.uk/postgate/witchposts.html (accessed April 2019; this page is no longer available).
17. Heather Pulliam, 'Blood, water and stone: the performative cross', in *Making Histories: Proceedings of the Sixth International Conference on Insular Art, York 2011* ed. Jane Hawkes (Donington: Paul Watkins, 2013). On the Cross as Tree of Life, see Barbara Beart (tr. Lee Preedy), *A Heritage of Holy Wood: The Legend of the True Cross in Text and Image* (Leiden: Brill, 2004).
18. Margaret Aston, *Broken Idols of the English Reformation* (Cambridge: Cambridge University Press, 2016).
19. Ursula Hall, *The Cross of St Andrew* (Edinburgh: Birlinn, 2006).
20. Crucifixes also sometimes have an X at the intersection of the arms, a result of mitred joints, as rays between the arms, or even as a specially applied mark, presumably representing Christ.

21. Nattrass, 'Witch posts'.
22. Ford, *Some Reminiscences*. See also www.northyorkmoors.org.uk/visiting/see-and-do/land-of-myths-and-legends (accessed November 2021).
23. *The North York Moors: A Guide to the North York Moors National Park* (North York Moors National Park, 1981) pp.11–12. Because the custom involved taking the coins out again, charged in a sense with the power of the Cross, it differed from the (largely modern) phenomenon of the coin tree.
24. Kate Thomas, 'The mark of Christ in wood, grass and field: open-air roods in Old English medical remedies', in *The Rood in Medieval Britain and Ireland, c.800–c.1500* ed. Philippa Turner and Jane Hawkes (Woodbridge: Boydell, 2020) pp.31–44.
25. Hayes and Rutter, *Cruck-framed Buildings*.
26. Arthur MacGregor, *Bone, Antler, Ivory & Horn: The Technology of Skeletal Materials Since the Roman Period* (London: Croom Helm, 1985) p.180.
27. Paul Stokes, 'A new interpretation of post-medieval bone scoops from the foreshore of the river Thames in London', in *Close to the Bone: Current Studies in Bone Technologies* ed. Selena Vitezović (Belgrade: Institute of Archaeology, 2016) pp.324–37.
28. Geoffrey Smaldon, 'Bone apple scoops', *Antique Collecting* 37(4) (2002) pp.40–3.
29. Stokes, 'A new interpretation'.
30. Clive Lloyd, *The Arts and Crafts of Napoleonic and American Prisoners of War 1756–1816* (London: Antique Collectors' Club, 2007) pp.117, 119.
31. Easton, 'Ritual marks' (1999); Easton, 'Ritual marks' (2000).
32. See for instance https://northyorkmoorsnationalpark.wordpress.com/2016/10/17/historical-curios-and-curious-patterns/ (accessed November 2021).
33. For purse bars, see Portable Antiquities Scheme (www.finds.org.uk) SUSS-295D53 and SUSS-C9EB44 (both from Sussex), and Ashmolean AN1950.295, illustrated in Standley, *Trinkets & Charms* p.63. For combs, MacGregor, *Bone, Antler, Ivory & Horn*.
34. Anne Teather and Andrew Chamberlain (2018) 'The chalk drums from Folkton and Lavant: measuring devices from the time of Stonehenge', *British Journal for the History of Mathematics* 34 (2018) pp.1–11; Anne Teather, Andrew Chamberlain and Mike Parker-Pearson, 'Getting the measure of Stonehenge', *British Archaeology* 165 (2019) pp.48–51
35. Sophie Oosterwijk, 'Chrysoms, shrouds and infants on English tomb monuments: a question of terminology?', *Church Monuments* 15 (2000) pp.44–64; Sophie Oosterwijk, 'Deceptive appearances: the presentation of children on medieval tombs', *Ecclesiology Today* 43 (2010) pp.45–60; there

is a summary in Roberta Gilchrist, *Medieval Life: Archaeology and the Life Course* (Woodbridge: Boydell, 2012) p.197.
36. James Hall, *Hall's Dictionary of Subjects and Symbols in Art* (revised edition, London: John Murray, 1979) p.119; James Hall, *Hall's Illustrated Dictionary of Symbols in Eastern and Western Art* (London: John Murray, 1994) p.66.
37. Chris Wood, 'Symbolic bindings', *Quest* 199 (2019) pp.19–23.
38. E.g. seen on a ninth-century silver mount found at Roudham, Norfolk: PAS (www.finds.org.uk) NMS-ADCA16.
39. See *Flags of the World*: www.crwflags.com/fotw/flags/index.html (accessed November 2021).
40. Hall, *Cross of St Andrew*.
41. Rebecca Ireland, 'Saint Michael the Archangel in pre-Reformation England, and implications for the 'butterfly cross' graffito', *Raking Light* (2018): https://rakinglight.co.uk/uk/saint-michael-the-archangel-in-pre-reformation- england-and-implications-for-the-butterfly-cross-graffito/ (accessed November 2021).
42. Geddes, *Decorative Ironwork*.
43. Lydia Greeves, *Houses of the National Trust* (London: National Trust Books, 2008) p.47.
44. John Timpson, *Timpson's England* (Norwich: Jarrold, 1987) pp.7, 100; Rhea, *Blessed Nicholas Postgate* pp.115–6.
45. Derek Bryce, *Symbolism of the Celtic Cross* (Felinfach: Llanerch, 1994) p.53.
46. Smaldon, 'Bone apple scoops'; Easton, 'Ritual marks' (1999); Easton, 'Ritual marks' (2000).
47. Catherine Yronwode, *Hoodoo in Theory and Practice: An Introduction to African-American Root Work*: www.luckymojo.com/hoodoo.html (accessed November 2021); Pennick, *Pagan Magic*.
48. Thomas Browne, *The Garden of Cyrus* (1658); Chris Wood, 'An alchemical nexus in seventeenth-century Norwich', *Quest* 195 (2018) pp.13–22.
49. Geddes, *Decorative Ironwork*.
50. Brian Hoggard, *Magical House Protection: The Archaeology of Counter-Witchcraft* (New York: Berghahn, 2019) p.91.
51. My thanks to Val Thomas for pointing out this last meaning. The rune can be seen as a vanishing point.
52. Stephen Mitchell, 'The n-rune and Nordic charms', in *'Viska alla vara välkomna!': Nordiska studier tillägnade Kristinn Jóhannesson* ed. Audur G. Magnúsdóttir et al. (Göteborg: Meijbergs Arkiv för Svensk Ordforskning, 2008) pp.219–29.
53. Christopher Alan Smith, *Icelandic Magic: Aims, Tools and Techniques of the Icelandic Sorcerers* (London: Avalonia, 2015).
54. Pennick, *Pagan Magic*.

Witchcraft and Counter-Magic in Early Twentieth-Century Cornwall

Jason Semmens

Editorial Note

At Hidden Charms 3, Jason Semmens spoke compellingly about his work on the early twentieth-century folklorist and curator William Henry Paynter. Since then he has prepared this research for the press, so that its publication in these Transactions isn't necessary. However, he has written the following notice of the book, which will appear as William Henry Paynter, ed Jason Semmens, *The Witchcraft and Folklore of Cornwall* (Privately published, 2024).

Whyler Pystry, 'Searcher-out of Witchcraft'

The South West has been a rich area for folklore fieldwork historically – Cornwall in particular. The folk tales of the region were the subject of one of the earliest printed collections, produced by Robert Hunt as *Popular Romances of the West of England: Or, The Drolls, Traditions, and Superstitions of Old Cornwall* (1865). The county's situation along the Atlantic-facing 'Celtic fringe' and mid-century nascent nationalist aspirations ensured that Cornwall's folklore became one of the key identifiers of its distinctive inheritance, along with its language and folk culture, which formed the focus of revival in the next generation. By 1920, this sense of Cornwall's 'Celtic' otherness led to the foundation of the Old Cornwall movement, with its motto 'Gather the fragments that are left that nothing be lost'. Members were encouraged to seek out and record the remaining 'fragments' of the native culture of Cornwall, considered to be in retreat in the face of modern advances in technology and societal changes as the twentieth century progressed. A number of individuals were actively engaged in folklore fieldwork under the aegis of the Old Cornwall movement during the inter-war years, but none were more keenly interested in the prevalence of witchcraft and the material culture relating to folk magic than William Henry Paynter (1901–1976) of Callington.

Around 1927 Paynter set out to record the folklore connected with witchcraft in East Cornwall, and he extended the scope of his researches to include the whole of the county. In 1930 Paynter noted that,

> About two years ago, I set myself the task of trying to obtain some of

> the witch stories associated with Cornwall. In so doing I have visited practically every parish in the county.
>
> I have discovered that witches and charmers, both male and female, exist today, and are looked up to and feared by the native population. There is a great deal more in witchcraft than people suppose. Strange and curious things do happen in the country, and I am strongly convinced that for many of them the witches are held responsible. I have interviewed people who believe that certain individuals acquire by direct compact with an evil spirit a certain amount of supernatural power, which is in general, though not always, employed to the prejudice of their neighbours or others who have incurred their displeasure.

Paynter sought and found examples of belief in witchcraft and folk magic in the more remote areas of Cornwall, principally amongst farmers, fishermen, and 'old dames', attesting to the vitality of popular belief in witchcraft as a cause of folk illness in Cornwall into the first half of the twentieth century. He also drew upon the researches and memories of other individuals involved in the Old Cornwall movement, particularly the fieldwork of Barbara C. Spooner of North Hill and Jim Thomas of Camborne, both of whom provided him with narratives relating to nineteenth-century cunning-folk and cases of bewitchment and unbewitchment in both East and West Cornwall. Paynter also used recent literary works to supplement these. Much of this material was collated into a succession of articles in the local and regional press during the 1920s and 30s which drew attention to beliefs many had assumed had long since waned, and on the strength of which he garnered national attention for the novelty of his research. Paynter was made a Bard of the Cornish Gorsedd in 1930 on account of his 'witch hunt' and rising media profile, taking the bardic name Whyler Pystry, 'Searcher-out of Witchcraft'.

In addition to folklore narratives, Paynter was able to secure and collect numerous examples of the material culture of folk magic – many apotropaic in nature, others of malign intent. As he related,

> In my so-called 'witch hunt' I have discovered the various sorts of the devil's agents, and have now before me as I write a collection of charms, &c., to ward off the effects of witchcraft, which I have collected in various parts of the county.

These items included double hazelnuts as prophylactics against toothache, a black bag containing bats' wings as a preservative against 'all terrors by night', several textual amulets including one containing a sigil taken from Scot's *Discovery of Witchcraft* (1584), the remains of a pig's heart pierced with pins, and the remains of 'Tammy Blee's Scent Bottle' obtained from a man whose late wife had originally acquired it as a love potion from the mid-nineteenth century cunning-woman Thomasine Blight (1793–1856). These artefacts were tangible links to the supernatural which Paynter had come to know through his narrative collections. As expressions of vernacular beliefs, they were material enough to be displayed in his home. One visitor to Paynter's abode in Callington was sufficiently impressed to recognise it as a 'necromantic museum'. Like his contemporaries collecting folklore, Paynter thought that the witch beliefs and folk-magic practices he encountered and collected were to be understood in terms of survivals, a doctrine which would give direct insight into pre-modern mentalities and systems of belief.

The wider world of the supernatural was also a source of fascination, especially the popular belief in the existance of ghosts. In addition to the first-hand accounts of sightings which Paynter collected from percipients, there were few haunted houses in East Cornwall that he did not visit in pursuit of a ghostly encounter. For example, he investigated the appearance of a Black Dog to several witnesses early in 1937 on a lonely stretch of road near Rilla Mill. The percipients attested to the dog's presence and its sudden disappearance, in spite of the high hedges bordering the lane. He employed the accoutrements of the ghost hunter's trade, popularised by the investigations of Harry Price, such as talcum powder and thermometers, but evidence for spectral manifestations eluded him, and in consequence Paynter maintained an ambivalent attitude to their possibility.

Paynter's practice as a folklore fieldworker was always that of an amateur, conducted in his spare time (his main employment was as a solicitors' general clerk). His lasting contribution is the corpus of West Country folklore he collected and preserved, and his personal witness to the steady dearth of belief in witchcraft as a source of illness in the South West of England. This decline began in the early twentieth century and accelerated after the Second World War. Paynter's articles in the local press chart the gradual disappearance of folk-magic practitioners curing supernaturally inflicted illness through these years, so that by 1969 he could state that 'witchcraft in its traditional form appears to have gone forever'. The persistence of charmers as purveyors of folk medicine remained undiminished, however, and as late as the 1950s he reported conducting research into charming traditions. The decline in supernatural beliefs from the seventeenth to twentieth centuries, as assumed from Max Weber's thesis of disenchantment, remains a focus for research and debate. Paynter's first-hand observations on the disappearance in Cornwall of practitioners focusing on folk illness, accompanied by the mid-century growth of interest in the occult, stands as testimony to changing social trends and beliefs.

Paynter's work also offers further opportunities for research since he is one of the few folklorists from the South West to have left a substantially complete archive of personal papers. Now dispersed between private and institutional collections, Paynter's extant manuscripts include draft versions of his unfinished and ultimately abandoned works, including a full length treatment of his researches into Cornish witchcraft dating from the late 1930s, and several chapters of a work on 'Cornish Ghosts and Other Strange Happenings' from the late 1940s. For various reasons these manuscripts failed to reach publication during Paynter's lifetime, and they remain as creative detritus within his archive. Along with the transactional papers, these literary works permit (with certain caveats) a more detailed and nuanced exploration of Paynter's folklore fieldwork than his published collections might suggest. Interrogation of his archive lies at the core of *The Witchcraft and Folklore of Cornwall*, to be published in January 2024. This book examines Paynter's research methods as revealed in his manuscript collections and places folklore collecting within the wider context of his activities and networks. It also considers Paynter's creative approaches to the material he encountered, particularly the interplay between oral and textual sources. Several of Paynter's manuscripts are included with critical apparatus.

The book includes a comprehensive bibliography of Paynter's published works, along with a chronology of his life and appendices on the media appearances which focused on his interest in folklore and the 'Cornish Museum' he curated in West Looe between 1959 and his death in 1976. The museum marked the culmination of Paynter's interest in the Old Cornwall movement, bringing together the fragmentary remains of the material culture of Old Cornwall that he had spent his life preserving for public display and instruction, and including the collection of witchcraft artefacts gathered years before on his 'witch hunt'.

Apotropaic Traces on Building Components: Beyond function and decoration

Marc Robben

Cruciferae

The cross-flower family (Cruciferae or Brassicaceae) is a worldwide plant genus known for its many edible species. The cruciferae got their name from the flower shape: four-petalled cross-shaped flowers that feature two long and two short stamens. The family supplies many of the winter vegetables such as cauliflower, kale, broccoli, Chinese cabbage, kohlrabi, bok choy, radishes, Brussels sprouts, watercress and white cabbage. Certainly our ancestors knew the cross-flowers very well.

From the middle of the twelfth century, the shape of church buildings changed with the transition from Romanesque to Gothic architecture. The ship became wider and higher. To let in more light, the windows had to be bigger. Ribbed vaults made it possible to realise larger spans. The outward thrust force (the horizontal pressure outwards, caused by the stone vaults and the roof) increased and concentrated in the piers between the windows.[1] The importance of stronger and larger buttresses was quickly apparent. The extra weight (vertical force component) reduced the horizontal pressure and made the oblique direction of the forces more and more vertical to transfer them to the foundations.

Fig. 1. Flowering Broccoli.

The master builders and masons had this basic sense of forces and pressures, but in the absence of any method of calculation, building was a matter of trial and error. Often part of a vault would collapse, or a roof, or walls. Practice taught them to go one step further in development and to provide the necessary stability by adjusting the buttresses or by using flying buttresses.

Fig. 2. Cathedral section 1: the flow of forces through the construction.

But what exactly was the cause when

something went wrong? Possibly it was not just about structural causes: after all, evil spirits were never far away. You can see, for example, that stone cross-flowers suddenly appear on the first supporting arches in the Gothic constructions. Three-dimensional crosses in stone were added. They consisted of a narrowing trunk (round or prismatic in shape), which ended in a ring or whorl and ended in four knobs or crockets. Certainly at that stage it seemed rather poor as a decorative addition. Yet in this way a vegetable cross was realized in three dimensions. The shape of the cross was visible from everywhere: sideways, from above, or from the ground floor. The flower, full of the power of nature, combined with the cross, the pre-eminent Christian symbol, to form a powerful magical weapon.

Fig.3. Cathedral section 2: cross-flowers on buttresses.

Flying buttresses underwent rapid architectural development in the late twelfth and early thirteenth centuries.[2] France took the lead in this. In Notre-Dame de Paris, the cathedral of Laon, and the Saint-Remi of Reims, the builders still used broad piers and flying buttresses that did not connect to the pressure points of the vaults and the roof. Form and logic improved at the cathedrals of Chartres (started 1195) and Soissons (started around 1200 and consecrated in 1212). The pillars of the choir were covered with gabled roofs, each provided with one finial, a cross-flower. The design evolved over the centuries from a Latin cross to a Lorraine or Orthodox cross, while the presence of stone cruciferae increased.[3]

On almost every ridge end of a church you will find a cross in many variants (some in iron and sometimes in stone). In many examples it is a cross-flower. This is even the case in my village church, which only dates back to 1865. Here solid finials are present on all ridge ends. These were the specific locations where symbols were needed to defend the place. However, the traditions in Britain diverged from those on the Continent.

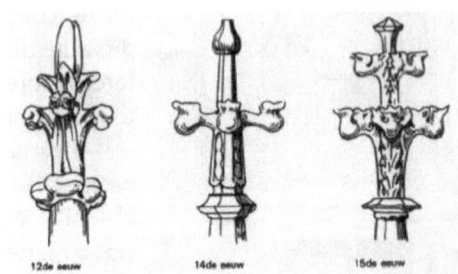

Fig.4. The evolution of the cross-flower motif.

Crockets

Crockets featured on flying buttresses or on eaves, usually in rows and decorated with leaves. At their first appearance in the late twelfth century, a crocket was a bullet-like knob with a spiral outline, similar to an unfurling frond. The crockets spread over the gable edges and rims as a natural protective overgrowth. In the later Gothic period they took the form of open, fully developed leaves, evolving into richly intricate shapes by the fifteenth century, more decorative than the solitary finials. The style details evolved: from less is more, to more is more. Their decorative value is indisputable. But wasn't an extra protection of natural forces useful?

Pinnacles

Builders knew the importance of buttresses. Their weight determined whether they could deflect the horizontal thrust forces enough to divert them to the foundations. Without sufficient mass (to increase the vertical force component), the roof and vaults (the horizontal component, the splash force) would push the church walls apart.

As the Gothic style evolved, buttresses were narrowed and the flying buttresses extended. The nave had to be bathed in light. But there were limits to the narrowing of buttresses. Where in the beginning the piers often reached higher than the foot of the flying buttresses (Soissons, Troyes), in later buildings pinnacles suddenly appear as the top finish of the buttresses.[4] They gracefully compensated for the diminished weight of the narrowed buttresses. The first such application of pinnacles can be found in the cathedral of Reims (from 1211), where they were nine metres high.

Pinnacles were already known from the Romanesque period, when they were used to make the top of the nave walls heavier. The name *pinnaculum*, 'highlight', came from Church Latin. They reached for heaven. Whether or not on a decorated column, they took the form of three-dimensional trees, square or octagonal in section, with edges full of crockets and with a finial on top. The power of nature bundled in stone. Was that referring to the oft-used protective tree of life?

The sketchbook of Villard de Honnecourt, compiled from 1235, is one of the oldest preserved documents with drawings of buildings.[5] It contains a drawing of the buttresses-pilasters of Reims Cathedral. De Honnecourt saw and drew the finials as crosses. In the same cathedral, the builders further completed the pilaster under the pinnacle with a guardian angel.[6] The *Spiegel Historiael* by Jocob Maerlant from 1284 contains a number of beautiful miniatures.[7] At least three of them show schematically represented buildings on which finials are visible. A miniature from the Rohan Hours (1418-1425) depicts how worldly ambitions – trade and money – threaten the church and the salvation of its faithful.[8] The drawing depicts the church as a besieged fortress, surrounded on all sides by a hostile world. Threatening waves and devastating fires attack the building from all sides and fiendish enemies tear down the pinnacles.

A magical surplus for protection. A mathematical formula would describe it this way: the force of nature multiplied by the Christian cross equals magic squared. A tree of life as a fertility symbol that reaches for the sky.[9]

In our Gothic cathedrals we see an abundance of finials and pinnacles. Though they are decorative, an apotropaic purpose seems defensible. They float in the waters of the gargoyles cut into the form of fearsome monstrosities, whose apotropaic character is quite generally accepted.[10]

Fig. 5. The Rohan Hours, 1418-1425.

The use of cross-flowers and pinnacles (in addition to the gargoyles) remained part of the Gothic architectural style. People may have looked at it differently, with their magical worldview. Demons were everywhere in battle array... No one knows for sure when the supposed protective aspect was forgotten in favour of the decorative.

As with the masonry marks, the English tradition went its own way. Here deviating variants were found in which the cross shape was sometimes less clearly visible. The evolution split into three successive style periods (Early English, Decorated, Perpendicular). In Oxford we find pinnacles topped with a crown instead of a finial. The king, head of the Anglican Church, as the ultimate patron?

The application of pinnacles was not a purely ecclesiastical matter. Older representations of Tattershall Castle in Lincolnshire showed finials on pinnacle-shaped finishes of the castle towers. They have disappeared in their current restoration. The castle of Martainville at Eure in Normandy was provided with pinnacles.

It is important to diversify interpretations in terms of place and time. When and where did people forget the apotropaic aim?

Succulent plants and roof ridges

House fire was a terrible disaster in the centuries when wood and straw were the standard building materials. Nothing was left to chance in order to protect goods, especially against lightning strikes. Farmers planted *Sempervivum tectorum*, house garlic or thunderblade, and *Sedum majus*, the evergreen house garlic, on their roofs. The iris flower (*lisca*, *lies* or *lis*) and the yellow iris (*Lis pseudacorus*) were also popular apotropaia.[11]

Succulents such as house garlic absorb a lot of moisture, can survive dry periods without any problems and are slow to catch fire. Sparks that rose from the fireplace and ended up on the roof were easily caught and extinguished by these succulents.

The ancient Greeks and Romans used to place house garlic on top of thatched roofs and it was used throughout Central and Western Europe as a defence against lightning and fire.[12] When Charlemagne discovered this tradition in southern France, he ordered in the *Capitulare de villis*, his estate ordinance of 812, that all his subjects should plant house garlic on their roofs as protection against lightning strikes: *et ille hortulanus habeat super domum suam Iovis barbam*, 'the gardener must have *Iovis Barbam* on top of his house'.

Iovis barbam, 'Jupiter's beard' (late *la joubarbe*) was the popular name in Romance-speaking areas. In the areas of Germanic language people referred to the thunder god Donar (cognate with the Norse Thor) so that in Germany the plant was called *donnerbart*.

In the Low Countries other roof plants were dedicated to Donar or to thunder itself (*donder* in Dutch) with names such as *donderbaard*, *donderbezem*, *donderkruid*, *dondertoppen*, *donderblaarkens*, *donderdistel*, *dondertoren* (*wilgenroosje*), *donderfak* and *donderbotten*.

The upright flowers of *Sempervivum*, punctuated by the wooden awls that pinned turves onto the top layer of thatch, formed a well-known roof ridge silhouette.

Would it be surprising if the horizontal ridge line of grander stone

Fig. 6. Roof ridge in the Open Air Museum, Bokrijk, Limburg.

buildings got decorated with elements of a similar shape? Viollet-le-Duc had already noticed this in his architectural encyclopedia where he described *la crête* and referred to the use of succulents: *l'origine des crêtes de comble se retrouve dans ce procedé naif* .[13] Admittedly, he considered the analogy functional rather than visual. He also described *la faitière*, the ridge line with examples of decorative tiles from the thirteenth century. The literature in the Low Countries refers to glazed roof ridges being installed from the fourteenth and fifteenth centuries. Old examples clearly resemble an iris plant or thunderweed. In Ghent, the remains of a fifteenth-century green-glazed ridge tile with a stylized iris plant were found.[14]

In the German Kannebakkersland (Westerwald) a folkloric tradition of decorative variations on this theme remained popular for a long time. Both the Dachplatte and the Fitstziegel were suitable elements for the application of all kinds of figures that were executed in a kind of carving technique: ordinary human figures, patron saints, symbolic defence signs, cross-with-heart and tree of life. Most remarkable were the whimsically sculpted and matt-glazed human and animal figures on the ridge or end-of-ridge tiles. Equestrian figures appeared on the ridge together with rushing horses, cocks, bowls, pentagrams against sorcery, witch's brooms and sun wheels. The perfection of craftsmanship subordinated itself to the preferentially chosen symbolic elements in which man could regain his confidence. Unfortunately, these examples have largely disappeared.

We are lucky that so many cathedrals and stately buildings have withstood the test of time. Their ridges, though worled in stone, seem to refer to the well-known silhouette of Sempervivum or other plants. The peak-shaped rhythm of plant shapes was often supplemented with finials. An apotropaic intention was not far away.

Today we still regularly find fired clay decorative ridges with motifs drawn from vegetation.[15] The variation in design is quite large. Sometimes a metal lightning defence was included as part of the product range. As more tiles were made in factories, the apotropaic input decreased and they evolved into decorative variants, to be chosen from a catalogue.

An apotropaic aim in addition to the functional and aesthetic purposes? Once again it seems important to diversify interpretations in terms of place and time. When and where did people forget the apotropaic aim? The continental tradition clearly differs from the British.

Sound
Noise is an important part of many actions to keep danger and evil spirits at

bay. Anyone who had to get something from the cellar as a child will probably remember the urge to make a noise as a reassuring signal against darkness and doom. Tinkling cow bells were originally supposed to protect the herd when it was without a keeper.[16]

A wind carillon – the first evidence of a wind chime – was found in an archaeological excavation in Southeast Asia. This dates from about 3000 BC; one of many primitive constructions of bone, wood or bamboo, stones or shells. It is believed that they served to ward off evil spirits. In Asia and the Mediterranean, they were used to simultaneously attract good spirits and ward off evil.[17]

Church bells were important. In 642 Pope John IV integrated church bells into the Catholic liturgy with an apotropaic function as well as that of summoning.[18] They sounded to drive away evil spirits while calling the faithful to church.[19] The devil was afraid of the chimes.[20] Bells were rung to chase away lightning and thunder.[21] Chimes, tinkles, the sound of bells and the tinkling of fluttering pipes work in the same way: they divert the attention of fairies, witches and devils from their original evil intentions. Church bells also functioned as an alarm signal against danger. It is still a Christian custom to consecrate the bells and to ring them at a wedding and a funeral.

The oldest bell from the Rhone region is in the church of Savigny (1527) and the oldest in the Loire in the church of Chalain-le-Comtal (1504). They bear the inscription *Vade retro Satanas et recognosce sententiam tuam et da honorem Deo vero et vero Filio*. This old formula, also used in exorcisms, begins with 'Get thee behind me, Satan'.[22] From the break with Catholicism in 1534 under Henry VIII, the Anglican Church broke with this custom. Between 1547 and 1549, she officially rejected the belief that consecrated bells were able to chase away devils.[23]

A large bell in the Grassmayrmuseum in Innsbruck bears the words: LAUDO DEUM VERUM – PLEBEN [sic] VOCO – CONCREGO CLERUN [sic] – DEFUNCTOS PLORO – PESTEM FUGO – FULMINA FRANGO – FESTA DECORO, 'I praise the true God, I call the people, I collect the clergy, I mourn the dead, I chase the plague, I break lightning, I adoern festivals'. Similar

Fig.7. Church bell, Grassmayrmuseum, Innsbruck.

inscriptions are found on a lot of old church bells. The inscription on the churchbell of Zonhoven (Limburg, België), dating from 1552, says *Quintinus es Mynen naem. Myn ghelut sy gode bequame. Also verre Men My hooren sal, wylt god bewaren over al*, 'My name is Quintinus (the parish saint). My sound be pleasing to God. The chime protects you as far as you can hear me'.

Some roof finials produced a whistling sound when the wind blew through them. There were endless ways to exorcise ghosts.

We are inclined to look for one meaning behind many insertions, decorations and representations. We should be aware that there can often be multiple intentions behind an object.[24] An apotropaic aim amongst other functions! The question is less whether the intention was also apotropaic than at what time people forgot this intention. The answer will probably differ in different locations.

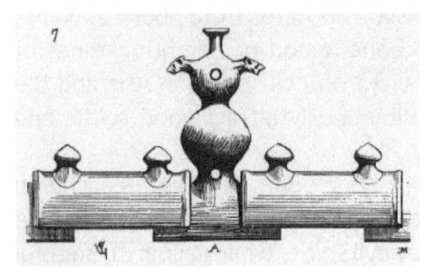

Fig.8. Roof tiles from Viollet-le-Duc's Encyclopédie.

Timber Framed Constructions with thatched roofs

Timber-framed buildings are usually constructed with vertical studs and horizontal beams. In the facades of rectilinear structures, some oblique connections are technically necessary as wind bracing. Compare it to a storage rack in wood or metal – without additional angled reinforcement, usually in the form of a metal cross-link at the rear, the rack can easily skew. Fig.9 shows a half-timbered construction with six slanting braces in the front. From a technical point of view, one or two braces per facade surface were sufficient. Because there were no methods of calculation at that time, and the carpenters were working with what was available, the final result could take all kinds of shapes. Sometimes wind-braces were repeated in a way that was unnecessary from a technical point of view, so that aesthetic appearance and symmetry may have played a role.

Fig.9. Timber-framing, Limburg, Belgium.

The braces were sometimes also elaborated with Andrew's crosses that ran over several horizontal bays. At the top of fig. 10 are some strut shapes especially common in German timber framing: the K-shape, the (wild) man, the Andrew's cross, intersecting curved struts and curved head struts.[25]

The common name 'wild man' and the (straight or curved) X-crosses show that structural features could sometimes play a symbolic role. Sometimes no bracing is visible.

There are various ways to infill the facade surfaces between the load-bearing structure: with a clay filling on a reinforcement of woven willow branches, or with masonry or a wood cladding. The fill could remain visible or be hidden under a layer of plaster. As the design of these facade sections was not dictated by the construction, there was room for individualised interpretation. Fashion and local customs played a role in this. This is certainly noticeable in the German half-timbered building tradition, as shown in the second and third rows of fig. 10. In many facades we recognize figures also found in apotropaic facade applications of masonry signs: Andrew's crosses, rhombuses, the combination of diamonds and Andrew's crosses and trees of life formed by wooden filler beams. Brick buildings were different. Here, various patterns were used, with alternating brick directions and sometimes different brick colours. Here too we sometimes recognize trees of life, inserted diamonds or an added heart.

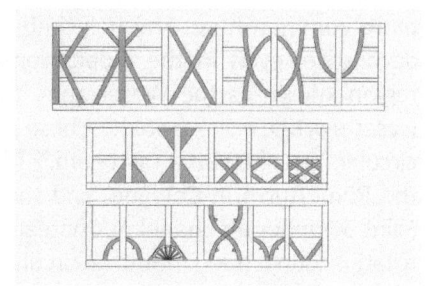

Fig. 10. Timber-framing designs, Germany.

Symbolic patterns in timber framing are more common in facades that are visible from the street. Elsewhere wind bracing is more often limited to what is needed for the construction. Here too we see a parallel with masonry marks. Every passerby had to be able to see that you were doing your bit in the fight against the ubiquitous ghosts, while owners wanted a facade that looked beautiful.

Why were x-crosses so emphatically applied? Like other signs in facades, they seem to straddle a dividing line between the decorative taking up of trends and a widely spread apotropaic reflex. Tree-of-life motifs (you can also see thunder brooms in them) were already recognized and mentioned in half-timbered buildings as apotropaic.[26] Why not, as long as the facade infill offered the possibility to better protect oneself against ghosts and evil. It was also nice if the result looked decorative. Often the symbol infills were added around facade openings or under the roofline, again pointing towards a possible apotropaion. Here too there is a clear evolution away from symbolism towards the decorative aspect. This phenomenon cannot be captured in black and white boxes.

German timber framing had a specific character. Diamond shapes were more common here. The half-timbered buildings were often colourful and decorative, even in the older examples. Around the River Weser, in the region known as the Weserraum, there are a striking number of rosettes (*rosette artige ornamentik*).[27] These solar motifs are semi-circular, sometimes circular, usually with a ray beam.[28] Identical motifs were already present on the Römerturm in Cologne, and they appear on old buildings such as the Saint Symphorien chapel at Château de Boussargues.[29] Other variants show rotating (sun wheel) motifs or circular patterns.

Clearly local trends mattered in timber frame construction. Of course, this did not rule out the possibility that latent apotropaic motifs could be associated with decoratively elaborated facade figures. There is little doubt about the more individually placed symbols near the facade openings of older buildings.

Just as old brick buildings may lack masonry marks, so there are many half-timbered buildings without visible symbols in their facades. The marks are more common in an urban environment. This may be due to the fear of fire, which was much greater in the densely built-up centres of towns, built in wood and roofed in thatch. Fires broke out in almost all cities, sometimes destroying an entire district.[30]

In terms of interpretation, it continues to dance on the vague division between aesthetic, creative, accidental forms and conjuring-protective purposes.

Fig. 11. The marketplace at Place Plumereau, Tours.

Notes
1. Richard Stemp, *De Symboliek van kerken en kathedralen, vorm en betekenis van de christelijke beeldentaal* (Alphen aan de Rijn: Icob BV, 2012) p.18.
2. Malcolm Hislop, *De Bouw van een kathedraal* (Kerkdriel: Librero, 2013) pp.64-9.
3. Wilfried Koch, *De Europese bouwstijlen* (Amsterdam: Agon, 1988).
4. Hislop, *De Bouw van een kathedraal* pp.70-1.
5. *The Sketchbook of Villard de Honnecourt*, ed Theodore Bowie (Bloomington IN: Indiana University Press, 1959).
6. Hislop, *De Bouw van een kathedraal* p.182.

7. Jacob van Maerlant, *Spiegel Historiael* ed Jozef Janssens and Martine Meuwese (Tielt: Davidsfonds, 1997) pp.44–7, 78–80, 160–3.
8. *Getijdenboek van Rohan* (Utrecht: Het Spectrum, 1973).
9. Koenraad Logghe, *Tussen hamer en staf, Voorchristelijke symboliek in de Nederlanden en elders in Europa* (Turnhout: Brepols, 1992) p.83.
10. Antoine Raguenet, *Gargoyles and Grotesques* (Dover Publications: New York, 2009); Alex Woodcock, *Gargoyles and Grotesques* (Oxford: Shire Library, 2011).
11. Clemens Trefois, *Het boerendak* (St-Niklaas: Danthe NV, 1980); Clemens Trefois, *Van vakwerk tot baksteenbouw* (St-Niklaas: Danthe NV, 1979); Clemens Trefois, *Ontwikkelingsgeschiedenis van onze Landelijke Architectuur* (St-Niklaas: Danthe NV, 1978).
12. Propser Janssens, 'Het oude verweer tegen hagel, donder en bliksem: II', *Oostvlaamsche Zanten* 6 (1957) pp.165–78.
13. Eugène Viollet le Duc, *Encyclopédie médiévale, d'après Viollet-le-Duc*, ed Georges Bernage (Bayeux: Editions Heimdal, 1978), pp.374–7, 496–8.
14. Clemens Trefois, *Ontwikkelingsgeschiedenis van onze Landelijke Architectuur* (St-Niklaas: Danthe NV, 1978) p.109.
15. Arie Schellingerhout, *Dakpannen, 2600 jaar Terracotta of keramische dakpan* (Leiden: Primavera Pers, 2009) pp.66–75.
16. Tensie Pellaerts and Eddy Geentjens, *Magie, hekserij en volksgeloof* (Kapellen: De Nederlandsche Boekhandel, 1986) pp.9–10.
17. https://artisanmoments.com/2018/07/30/wind-chimes-an-origin-story/ #:~:text=3000%20B.C.%2D%20Natural%20wind%20chimes,of%20man's %20first%20musical%20instruments, accessed December 2021.
18. Alfons Roeck and Léon Marquet, *Belgische sagen en legenden* (Antwerp: De Vlijt, 1980) pp.139–40.
19. Janssens, 'Het oude verweer tegen hagel, donder en bliksem'.
20. Jos Schrijnen, *Nederlandsche Volkskunde* (Arnhem: Gysbers & Van Loon, 1977) p.123.
21. Alfons Roeck, *Vlaamse Volkscultuur, Het traditionele volksleven* (Deurne: Baert, 1982) p.120.
22. Jacques Collin de Plancy, *Dictionnaire infernal* (sixth edition, Paris: Henri Plon, 1863) p.174.
23. 23. Keith Thomas, *Religion and the Decline of Magic: Studies in Popular Beliefs in Sixteenth- and Seventeenth-Century England* (London: Weidenfeld & Nicolson, 1971) p.34, bells rung against 'great thundering' in Sandwich, 1502 and 1514; p.65, dismissed by reformers.
24. Marc Robben, *Magische gebouwbescherming, Tussen Magie en Decoratie* (Privately published, 2021).
25. Heinrich Stiewe, *Fachwerk Häuser in Deutschland* (Darmstadt: WBG, 2015)

p.19.
26. Clemens Trefois, *Van vakwerk tot baksteenbouw* (St-Niklaas: Danthe NV, 1979) p.103–14.
27. Wilhelm Hansen and Herbert Kreft, *Fachwerk im Weserraum* (Hameln: Niemeyer, 1980).
28. Stiewe, *Fachwerk Häuser in Deutschland*.
29. https://www.boussargues.com/histoire/la-chapelle, accessed December 2021.
30. Willy Dezutter and Marc Ryckaert, *Brandgevaar en bouwvoorschriften in de Middeleeuwen – een vroeg Vlaams voorbeeld: Aardenburg 1232* (Middelburg: Archief Zeeuw Genootschap, 1976).

Tower of Strength: Buildings archaeology and apotropaic symbols in medieval elite society

James Wright

Sacred and Secular

Research across the last two decades has gone far to suggest that there was significant cross-pollination between sacred and secular architecture during the medieval period.[1] Perhaps this should not be a great surprise in an age where secular lords patronised sacred buildings and clerics of the upper rank often lived a high-status existence in castles and great houses.[2] The same craftspeople were often employed to work on both sacred and secular buildings and transferred their experience, knowledge and skills between building sites.[3]

The overriding architectural symbol of authority, both spiritual and temporal, was the tower. Elite landscapes were dominated by the twin focus of church and castle towers. This can be seen at lordly level through the building of the adjacent manor house and parish church at Strelley (Nottinghamshire) for Sir Sampson de Strelley. At the rank of an earl, it is visible in the construction of the castle and monastery at Castle Acre (Norfolk) for William de Warenne. At the highest stage of society, the multi-phased works at both the Palace Westminster and Westminster Abbey – from the reign of Edward the Confessor through to that of Henry VII – demonstrate the continued importance of these locations to the monarchy. All these contiguous buildings featured towers, a factor which has led Philip Dixon to characterise the tower as *'a shell for the overt symbolism of social power'*.[4]

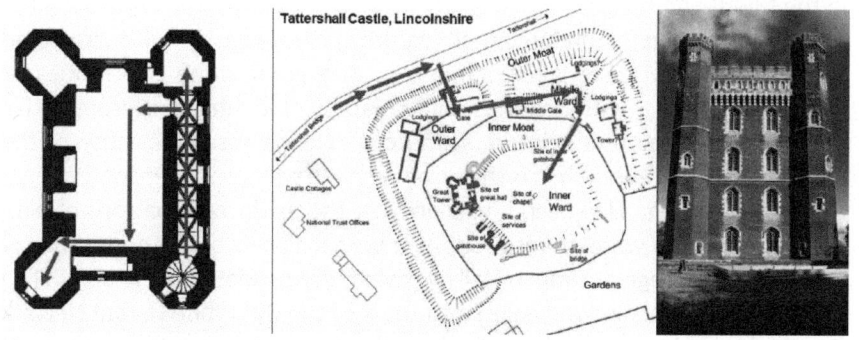

Fig. 1. Ground plan of Tattershall Castle (Lincolnshire) showing the circuitous route through the various gates (centre), the processional access to the second floor of the great tower (left) and the western show-front of the great tower (right).

Access to the great tower of a castle – the ultimate symbol of lordship – was often deliberately circuitous. This phenomenon was not usually connected to defensive fortification but was intended to theatrically heighten the ceremonial approach to the presence of a magnate. Coming to fifteenth-century Tattershall Castle (Lincolnshire), from the south-west, travellers would be confronted by a show-front consisting of five towers. In the background were several other gate towers, mural towers, and the tower of the collegiate church. This scene was dominated by the principal west elevation of the 33.5-metre-high great tower. On entering the outer gate of the castle, the visitor would have a stark view of the north elevation of the great tower, but this perspective altered with the east elevation gradually coming into view as the traveller passed through the middle and inner gates. However, the journey was still not complete as, once within the Inner Ward, the visitor had to negotiate first the screens passage of the great hall and then a secondary corridor before access was granted to the great tower. After climbing an impressively engineered spiral stair, the visitor to the second floor would be guided into the second-floor apartments, along a lengthy vaulted corridor, and then into an antechamber to await summons by the Lord Treasurer of England – Ralph Lord Cromwell. When that order arrived, the theatre continued with Cromwell presented at the high end of his great chamber beneath a tester canopy, floodlit by enormous tracery windows, sitting close to a fireplace covered in sculpted motifs that announced his ancient pedigree.[5] Tattershall was not alone in such stage-managed entrances. When considering similar access routes to castles such as Bodiam and Kenilworth, Matthew Johnson concluded that 'it is difficult to avoid the conclusion that the overall effect is that of a liturgical procession; religious and secular worlds are never far away in the Middle Ages'.[6]

In the design of architectural features, the language of sacred and secular can be visually indistinguishable. The great stone doorframes at Tattershall Castle – with deeply moulded jambs, flat lintels enclosing gothic arches and cusped motifs in the spandrels – closely resemble those of the adjacent collegiate church. It is the same with the window tracery of the great tower and church.[7] However, it was not just the aristocratic patrons of elite architecture who were so inspired. At a vernacular level the doorframe of the screens passage at Dragon Hall, Norwich, the window tracery at 42 High Street, Winchester, and the painted statuary of the Old White Hart at Newark (Nottinghamshire) all use forms that would be equally appropriate in a late medieval church. Such choices demonstrate an element of social aspiration among lower ranking secular patrons familiar with the detailing common in ecclesiastical architecture.

This interplay between the sacred and secular is visible in both elite and non-elite architecture. But what of the discreet motifs formally incorporated or informally inscribed on the walls of those buildings? Is it also present in these? Historic graffiti studies have established that a significant percentage of the recorded assemblage can be typologically categorised as apotropaic.[8] Such informal graffiti – probably intended to ward off evil, simultaneously averting bad luck and bringing good luck to a building – have been surveyed in locations connected both to both the natural world (trees, caves) and the built environment (ecclesiastical buildings, high status residences and vernacular structures).[9] Common motifs include pentagrams, circular designs and VV or M inscriptions. On examining apotropaic graffiti, it appears that all three of these types may have their original inspiration in the formal artwork patronised by medieval elites in both sacred and secular contexts.

Fig. 2. The Old White Hart, Newark (Nottinghamshire).

Holy Symbols: Pentagram and Rosette Designs

There are several reasons why the pentagram might be found adorning the walls of a medieval building. Some, very limited, evidence suggests that a small number of master builders favoured it within the geometrical procedures of their designs; it can appear as a stonemason's mark; and it may be informally carved as an apotropaic graffito.[10] Examples of the latter include those recorded during surveys at St Mary's Troston (Suffolk), Holy Trinity Tattershall (Lincolnshire) and St James' Aslackby (Lincolnshire). It has been frequently pointed out that the pentagram was an important holy symbol in the Middle Ages. This was outlined in a passage of *Sir Gawain and the Green Knight* where the poet digresses, at length, about why Gawain had pentagrams on his shield and garb. Much of this was linked to Christian numerology on the number five (five flawless senses, five faultless fingers, five wounds of Christ, five joys of Mary and five knightly virtues) but the author also emphasised that the shape itself had power, 'through the endless line a five pointed form which never failed'.[11] Furthermore, it is made clear in the poem that the pentagram was specifically associated with the biblical king Solomon. Jewish tradition, adopted in turn by the other Abrahamic faiths, told how God gave Solomon a powerful brass and iron seal ring which had the power to repel demons. The ciphers which gave the ring its power were not relayed in the Jewish tradition, but the symbol was interpreted as a six-pointed star within Islam and a five-pointed star within western Christianity.[12]

This belief system led to the incorporation of the pentagram as a motif within churches by master builders and their clerical patrons.[13]

Fig. 3. West window of Exeter Cathedral.

Masons working at Holy Trinity Hull, c.1400, included a label stop featuring an angel clutching a shield emblazoned with a pentagram – a scene reminiscent of Gawain's own shield. Elsewhere, there is a vast pentagram visible in the mid-fourteenth century tracery of the great west window at Exeter Cathedral. A near-contemporary building of c.1320–90, the Marktkirche at Hannover (Lower Saxony), has a brick west tower with a huge pentagram picked out within the eastern gable. The incorporation of these pentagrams into medieval design schemes was not left to accident; they must have been deliberately included as apotropaic art, sanctioned by the church authorities. If the pentagram was part of mainstream medieval poetic and spiritual culture, then it would make sense for it to be co-opted as informal graffiti. Such inscriptions could have been the work of builders, occupants, or visitors to buildings keen to protect themselves, their interests, and their structures from the threat of evil.

Another motif which has a varied catalogue of interpretation is the six-pointed rosette – sometimes referred to as the daisywheel, hexafoil or flower of life. Many cultures have included this symbol within their iconography, but for medieval Europeans it was important in geometrical construction, had an apotropaic function and could be used as an alternative to the cross. In the Anglo-Norman period, rosette designs were commonly associated with the Crucifixion and often stand in for the Cross or appear in association with crosses.[14] Examples can be found on tympana of the eleventh and twelfth centuries including those at St Mary and All Saints Hawksworth (Nottinghamshire), St Leonard's Scarcliffe (Derbyshire) and St Andrew's Bredwardine (Herefordshire). Elsewhere, the motif was carved on church fonts including those at St Mary and All Saints Sculthorpe (Norfolk), St Nonna Altarnum and St Michael Landrake (Cornwall). The apotropaic nature of the rosette in tympanum and font is there by inference – one related to fears of the penetration of evil forces through a vulnerable portal, the other connected to the rejection of the Devil during the baptismal sacrament.

Such designs had a longevity which certainly continued within ecclesiastical art beyond the Anglo-Norman period, as exemplified in the early fourteenth-century flint flushwork of the Ethelbert Gate at Norwich Cathedral and within the late fifteenth-century spandrels of the tomb brass of Ralph Lord Cromwell and Margaret Deincourt at Holy Trinity Tattershall. The rosette was even transferred to portable goods such as the ampullae, containing holy water brought home by pilgrims, examples of which have been found at Bagworth (Leicestershire) and Watton (East Yorkshire), both dated by the Portable Antiquities Scheme to c.1350–1530.

Rosettes can also be found in secular art. The motif was included on the cheek-piece of a helmet in the collection at Arundel Castle (West Sussex) and was depicted on the poleyns of the *Young Knight in a Landscape* by Vittore Carpaccio. Stamping protective imagery onto armour seems a good spiritual solution for soldiers at risk of physical harm. It can be mirrored by the incorporation of the IHS christogram on the sword scabbard of William de Roos' tomb effigy at St Mary's Bottesford (Leicestershire). Elsewhere, rosettes appear on other elite items including the carved faces of sixteenth century chests in the collections at Rockingham Castle (Northamptonshire) and Haddon Hall (Derbyshire). In the late seventeenth century there may even have been a direct dialogue between a carved rosette on the lid of a chest held at Holme Pierrepont Hall (Nottinghamshire) and multiple graffiti on the surrounding timberwork. Is it possible that the formally carved motif gave licence and inspiration to the informal graffiti?

Fig. 4. St Ethelbert's Gate, Norwich.

Archaeological survey has indicated that a great many graffiti rosettes may be related to folk traditions connected with the protective power of the endless line, also found in designs such as pentagrams, knots, meshes, and circles.[15] Thousands of apotropaic rosettes have been recorded across England such as those at Colchester Castle (Essex), St Mary's Cheltenham (Gloucestershire), St Mary's Happisburgh (Norfolk), St Wilfrid's Kelham (Nottinghamshire) and

York Minster. Just as the pentagram was used both formally and informally, so the rosette appealed to elite and non-elite audiences alike, in both secular and sacred contexts.

The rosette motif was favoured for a surprisingly long time. Recent graffiti surveys have found it employed in the buck of Kibworth Harcourt Windmill (Leicestershire), which post-dates 1773, and also in the coach house at Holme Pierrepont Hall (Nottinghamshire) which was constructed after 1875.[16] The purpose of symbols can alter over time and space, so it is by no means certain that rosettes in the eighteenth- or nineteenth-century East Midlands had the same meaning as when they were used as an alternative to the cross in Anglo-Norman tympana. Although rosettes may have been imbued with specific holy power during the medieval era, by the time the windmill was built at Kibworth Harcourt they could simply have been carved to bring good luck to a building whilst keeping bad luck at bay.

The Great Debate: M and VV Motifs
The presence of M's and conjoined V's has been acknowledged in historic graffiti studies over the last two decades. They are commonly found during surveys at medieval buildings including St Nicholas Sevenoaks (Kent), St Albans Abbey, St Botolph's Trunch (Norfolk), St Mary's Lowdham (Nottinghamshire) and Lincoln Cathedral. The problem lies in assigning specific dates to graffiti which could have been inscribed at any point after the construction of the building. However, enough securely dated examples have been identified to indicate that the inscriptions were common in the medieval period. An early advocate for their apotropaic interpretation was Timothy Easton who thought that they were Marian symbols – the initial M standing for *Maria* (Mary, the Mother of God), the VV for *Virgo Virginum* (Virgin of Virgins, said to be a reference to a Catholic sung lament).[17] More recently, Matthew Champion has queried this interpretation in the light of what he has called 'big data' – analysis of graffiti initials which indicates a post-medieval popularity for Christian names beginning with the letters M and W.[18] However, Champion has previously noted that VV marks may, in certain medieval contexts, be related to the Marian cult, and he drew attention to the use of formally carved conjoined V's on the west elevation of St Peter and St Paul Fakenham (Norfolk).[19]

Close analysis of the Fakenham frontage shows, flanking the sill of the west window, a crowned VV and a crowned M. The latter is a common symbol representing Mary as Queen of Heaven and is frequently found at churches including St Martin's Fincham (Norfolk), Holy Trinity Blythburgh (Suffolk) and All Saints Hawton (Nottinghamshire). The presence of the crown over the VV at Fakenham would suggest that, in this specific context, the symbol is also Marian. Its devotional context is confirmed by adjacent features including two niches which once contained religious statuary, a row of eight crowned D's standing for *Dominus* (the Lord) and numerous armorials. The latter are another indicator of the overlap between the sacred and the secular. They reflect an age where outward expressions of piety were an important marker of elite status through the patronage of ecclesiastical construction.

Conjoined V motifs occur elsewhere in late medieval English art and architecture. Fifteenth-century examples can be seen carved in stone within the quatrefoil of blind tracery at Christchurch Priory and on the exterior of the chapel stair turret at Haddon Hall (Derbyshire). A timber example exists on the finial of a bench-end at Holy Rood Buckland Newton (Dorset) and the motif can also be found in the paintwork on the pulpit at St Mary and All Saints Fotheringhay (Northamptonshire). Portable instances of the VV symbol also occur. The ampulla from Watton, referred to above with its rosette design, also has conjoined V's on its opposite face. Elsewhere, lead tokens with VV's on them have been found at Clipstone and Broxtowe (Nottinghamshire). These portable objects were probably not especially high-status examples of the motif and show that, as with pentagrams and rosettes, Marian symbols were popular across society.

Fig. 5. Conjoined V's on the exterior of the chapel stair turret at Haddon Hall (Derbyshire).

Medieval elite patrons used Marian imagery to project and boost their status through shows of piety. The architectural examples above all come from ecclesiastical buildings but there are cases from secular structures too. Innovative brickmasons working on the great tower at Tattershall Castle c.1431–51 included diaperwork which picked out geometrical patterns such as lozenges and lattices using the overfired burnt ends of bricks. Tattershall was one of the first major secular structures to incorporate diaperwork and has what is almost certainly the first pictorial instance on its western show-front. Between the third-floor windows is a diaperwork shield – a symbol of secular lordship – beneath which is an M lying between the second-floor windows. These two spaces contained Ralph Cromwell's great chamber and bedchamber, his principal suites of accommodation, so the twin associations of armorial and Marian imagery were strong outward expressions of his pious lordship. These statements were reinforced through diaperwork conjoined V's placed directly above an M in the brickwork of the south-west turret.[20]

In later structures, such as the Lower School at Eton College and the great tower at Buckden Palace (Lincolnshire), diaperwork crosses can be identified in buildings with pseudo-ecclesiastical status. Meanwhile, at Kirby Muxloe Castle (Leicestershire), William Lord Hastings ordered brickmasons to pick out designs which included his initials and his personal livery badges of a maunche, a ship and a knight – entirely secular themes. Perhaps Ralph Cromwell was alone in using the medium to harness sacred and secular power together, yet it was moments such as this which led Margaret Aston to declare that 'boundaries of place did not separate religious and secular images'.[21] Whilst it is now impossible to gain a direct understanding of Cromwell's personal Christianity, we can be reasonably certain that he wished the viewer present and future to consider him a great and pious lord when they saw the motifs projected upon his great tower. The structure was the ultimate symbol of Cromwell's lordship – it was a tower of strength with an incredibly complex access that not only recalled ecclesiastical processions but was also emblazoned with devotional imagery. That some of those symbols could have fulfilled an apotropaic function may have appealed to a man who was often concerned with the perceived righteousness of his actions.[22]

Fig. 6. Conjoined V's and an M motif picked out in diaperwork on the great tower at Tattershall Castle. [Image edited to enhance the pattern]

Fig. 7. Tattershall Castle – Ralph Cromwell's tower of strength.

Conclusions

Sacred perspectives played a very important part in all aspects of medieval life.

However, the demarcation between sacred and secular was not as rigid to the medieval mind as it is to the modern one. Consequently, it is possible to find many places where expressions of elite lordship intrude upon ecclesiastical settings, and others where piety is articulated in the great houses of temporal lords. This architecture can be read as the social expression of those who patronised the buildings and many of those structures are deliberately implanted with motifs which seem to have apotropaic and devotional purposes. The pentagram is a device well-documented as a repeller of evil: to encounter it at Exeter Cathedral can leave us in no doubt that apotropaic symbols were part of the lexicon of the mainstream Catholic church. If the pentagram is then found as graffiti, it is reasonable to conclude that its purpose may often have been an informal expression of religious orthodoxy. Here we may be seeing a transmission of ideas from formal art to informal graffiti, similar to the transference of architectural features from the churches and castles of the elite to humbler vernacular buildings.

The clerical function of the rosette and Marian imagery was perhaps slightly different in purpose – here we find more devotional symbolism, connected respectively with the adoration of the Cross and the cult of the Mother of God. However, the motifs were – by their very nature – holy symbols, resonant and sacred. To find those self-same symbols repeated as inscriptions, frequently in contexts which imply an apotropaic function, indicates that there may have been a dynamic and fluid relationship between medieval artistic expression and graffiti.

Notes

1. For example: Kent Rawlinson, '"In chapel, oratory or other suitable places in their houses": religious routines and the residences of greater medieval households' in *The Medieval Great House* ed. Malcolm Airs and Paul Barnwell (Donington: Shaun Tyas, 2011) pp.171–99; Sarah Speight, 'Religion in the bailey: charters, chapels and the clergy' in *Chateau Gaillard 21, La Basse-cour: Actes du colloque international de Maynooth, 2004*, ed Anne Marie Flambard Hericher, Peter Ettel, and Tom McNeill (Caen: Publications du CRAHM, 2004) pp.271–80; Margaret Aston, 'The use of images' in *Gothic: Art for England,1400–1547* ed. Richard Marks and Paul Williamson (London: V&A Publications, 2003) pp.68–75; Matthew Johnson, *Behind the Castle Gate* (London: Routledge, 2002) pp.19–54, 83.
2. Mick Aston, *Monasteries in the Landscape* (Stroud: Tempus, 2000) pp.63–78; Michael Welman Thompson, *Medieval Bishops' Houses in England and Wales* (Aldershot: Ashgate, 1998).
3. It is clear from the building accounts of Kirby Muxloe Castle (Leicestershire)

that the master stonemason John Cowper was also simultaneously working on the collegiate church of Holy Trinity at Tattershall (Lincolnshire) for separate patrons – Bishop William Waynflete at Tattershall and William Lord Hastings at Kirby Muxloe; see Alexander Hamilton Thompson, 'The building accounts of Kirby Muxloe Castle: 1480–84', *Transactions of the Leicestershire Archaeological Society* 11 (1913–20) pp.193–345 at p.200.
4. Philip Dixon and Beryl Lott, 'The courtyard and the tower: contexts and symbols in the development of late medieval great houses', *Journal of the British Archaeological Association* 146 (1993) pp.93–101 at p.99.
5. James Wright, 'Tattershall Castle: Building a History', unpublished PhD thesis, University of Nottingham (2021) pp.59–61, 91–6, 107–9.
6. Johnson, *Behind the Castle Gate* p.83.
7. Wright, 'Tattershall Castle: Building a History' pp.70, 93, 97.
8. Matthew Champion, *Medieval Graffiti – The Lost Voices of England's Churches* (London: Ebury Press, 2015) p.25.
9. For arborglyphs (trees), Richard Reeves and I recorded several unpublished examples in the New Forest during the summer of 2015; for caves, Chris Binding and Linda Wilson, 'Ritual protection marks in Goatchurch Cavern, Burrington Combe, North Somerset', *Proceedings of the University of Bristol Speleological Society* 23 (2004) pp.119–33; for churches, Champion, *Medieval Graffiti* pp.23–60; for great houses, James Wright, 'Cultural anxieties and ritual protection in high-status early modern houses' in *Hidden Charms – a conference held at Norwich Castle, April 2nd 2016* ed. John Billingsley, Jeremy Harte and Brian Hoggard (Mytholmroyd: Northern Earth, 2017) pp.71–81; for vernacular structures, Linda Hall, *Period House Fixtures and Fittings: 1300–1900* (Newbury: Countryside Books, 2005) pp.150–3.
10. Robert Bork, *The Geometry of Creation – Architectural Drawing and the Dynamics of Gothic Design* (London: Routledge, 2011) p.12; Champion, *Medieval Graffiti* pp.45–52; *Mediaeval Mythbusting Blog #11: The Pentagram*, https://triskeleheritage.triskelepublishing.com/mediaeval-mythbusting-blog-11-pentagram/ (accessed December 2021); *Mediaeval Mythbusting Blog #12: Stonemason's Marks*, https://triskeleheritage.triskelepublishing.com/mediaeval-mythbusting-blog-12-stonemasons-marks/ (accessed December 2021).
11. *Sir Gawain and the Green Knight*, tr. Simon Armitage (London: Faber & Faber, 2007) p.35.
12. Joseph Jacobs and Max Seligsohn, 'Seal of Solomon' in *The Jewish Encyclopaedia* ed Isidore Singer (New York: Funk & Wagnalls, 1906), p.448.
13. Imagery in churches was never left entirely at the discretion of the builders. It was made clear at the second Council of Nicea in 787 that the

church fathers took an active interest in setting the agenda for artistic representation in churches; see Emile Mâle, *Religious Art in France, XIII Century: A Study of Medieval Iconography and its Sources*, tr Dora Nussey (London: J.M. Dent, 1913) p.392. Clearly, this directive continued to have an impact because, as late as 1306, the bishop of London instructed the prior of Holy Trinity Aldgate to investigate the acquisition of a crucifix at St Mildred's Poultry which was in some way unconventional and therefore proscribed; see George Gordon Coulton, *Social Life in Britain from the Conquest to the Reformation* (Cambridge: Cambridge University Press, 1956) p.473.
14. Champion, *Medieval Graffiti* pp.39-40.
15. Champion, *Medieval Graffiti* pp.29-60; Timothy Easton, 'Apotropaic symbols and other measures for protecting buildings against misfortune', in *Physical Evidence for Ritual Acts, Sorcery and Witchcraft in Christian Britain: A Feeling for Magic* ed. Ronald Hutton (Basingstoke: Palgrave Macmillan, 2015) pp.39-67 at pp.47-50; Brian Hoggard, *Magical House Protection: The Archaeology of Counter-Witchcraft* (New York: Berghahn, 2019) pp.74-86.
16. James Wright, 'Historic Graffiti Survey of Kibworth Harcourt Windmill, Leicestershire', unpublished archaeological report, Triskele Heritage (2021) pp.14-15; Matt Beresford, 'Historic Graffiti at Holme Pierrepont Hall, Nottinghamshire – Survey Report', unpublished archaeological report, MB Archaeology (2021) p.7.
17. Timothy Easton, 'Ritual marks on historic timber', *Weald and Downland Open Air Museum Journal* (Spring 1999) pp.22-8 at pp.24-5; Easton, 'Apotropaic symbols' pp.41-3.
18. *Which Marks? Those Marks... The Case for Ritual Protection in Medieval Graffiti*, https://www.youtube.com/watch?v=jV9i_mtTyuE (accessed December 2021).
19. Champion, *Medieval Graffiti* p.56.
20. Wright, 'Tattershall Castle: Building a History' pp.121-2.
21. Aston, 'The use of images' p.72.
22. James Wright, 'Tattershall Castle and the newly-built personality of Ralph Lord Cromwell', *Antiquaries Journal* 101 (2021) pp.301-32.

Where there's Muck, there's Magic: Recording meaningful marks in Peak District farm buildings

Andy Bentham

This paper presents findings from the recording of marks and symbols found within traditional farm buildings of the Peak District. Most frequently recorded were scribed circular designs and flame-shaped burn or scorch marks. Whilst the purpose of these marks in farm buildings remains open to debate, they are both currently considered to have been made with meaning and purpose and are broadly thought to have been protective, perhaps warding against misfortune and keeping buildings, stored crops and valuable livestock safe from harm.

The recording has established that the use of such marks was widespread across the region, far from uncommon and continued at least until the very late 19th century.

A motivation for recording

In the Peak District traditional farm buildings contribute greatly to the landscape, but most are unsuited for today's farming methods. Consequently, many have been developed and found new uses, whilst others have fallen into disrepair. Surviving original interior surfaces are being lost as are the various fixtures and fittings, and along with them any inscribed markings. In 2015 when considering the occurrence of circular marks in barns and stables, Timothy Easton described a 'particular urgency to record evidence for each part of Britain'.[1] Without such recording, the physical evidence of mark-making in vernacular farm buildings will disappear and the real extent of this practise will never be known.

Fig. 1. As interior surfaces are lost, along with them go any inscribed marks. Here at Knouchley Farm, Calver, part of a six-petalled rosette or hexafoil remains hanging on, the rest having fallen away.

The Peak, its farm buildings and recording marks

The Peak District is a predominantly upland area at the foot of the Pennines, much of which was designated as Britain's first national park in 1951. It is an area where historic farmsteads have survived well and is rich in traditional buildings, most of which were built before 1900.[2] Buildings are grouped in the small farmsteads typical of upland areas, but more isolated outfarms and field barns are also common. Within the farmstead there can be a range of building types, with housing for cattle and the storage of winter fodder of particular importance.[3]

Fig. 2. Field Barns near Longnor, Staffordshire Moorlands. Traditional farm buildings make a valuable contribution to the character of the Peak District.

Recording in the Peak District began informally in 2015, but has developed in scale since then. It is still ongoing and as more buildings are visited and increasing numbers of marks are documented, it becomes possible to identify patterns and local variations.

Once a suitable building has been identified for recording and access arranged, the simple process of carefully inspecting interior surfaces with strong LED lighting can be surprisingly revealing. In addition to working construction marks and the graffiti left by generations of farm workers, the potentially meaningful marks are sometimes found. Some are quite obvious and building owners are aware of them, others are so lightly inscribed they appear insignificant, going unnoticed for decades or more.

Fig.3. Examining surfaces in a hayloft: without using lighting, some marks simply could not be seen.

To date, some 29 farm buildings in the Peak District have been identified with one or more circular marks, while burn marks have been documented in 20 locations. Several farmsteads have marks in more than one building and in some cases, such as Brushfield Hough near Taddington, both burn marks and circular designs have been recorded, but in different buildings of the yard. So far, there are only two buildings in which both types of mark occur together (see Fig. 11).

With surviving traditional farmsteads, outfarms and field barns numbering in the thousands, only a very small percentage of the existing buildings can have been visited.[3] From what has been found so far, there can be no doubt that many more buildings in the region will have significant marks.

Circular designs

Inscribed circular marks have a long history in buildings of many types. They have been recorded across the country in large numbers, particularly during surveys of early church graffiti.[4] They have been widely discussed as protective or apotropaic symbols, used to avert evil and bad luck.[5]

In many counties, circular marks are found in farm buildings; numerous examples have been published by Timothy Easton.[6] Whilst many marks appear to be of the eighteenth and nineteenth centuries, earlier examples seem to suggest a long-standing association with agricultural buildings.[7] Full-scale surveys such as that of the monastic barn at Bradford on Avon have shown how a single agricultural building may contain very large numbers of circular designs.[8] Examples continue to be identified during formal historic building assessments and with ever-increasing public awareness, growing numbers are reported via the various social media platforms. Despite this, marks in farm buildings remain under-recorded nationally.

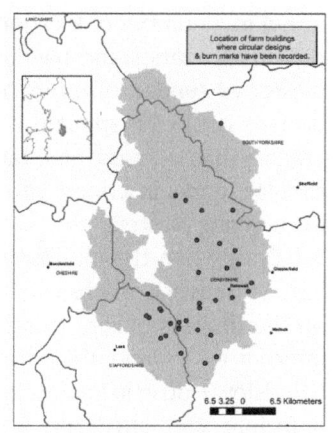

Fig. 4. The Peak District National Park.

The circular designs recorded in the Peak appear to have been created with a tool like carpenter's dividers and are made up of circles typically some 200mm to 300mm across, though diameters range from 25mm to around 600mm. Designs include plain circles, concentric circles and groups of overlapping or intersecting circles. Incomplete designs and partial circles are common. Geometric circular marks with varying numbers of internal arcs are frequent, including the ubiquitous hexafoil, a rosette design of six internal arcs. Versions using four and twelve arcs are also regularly seen. In some cases, a scribed circle is divided by straight lines rather than arcs scribed by a divider, as is more usual.

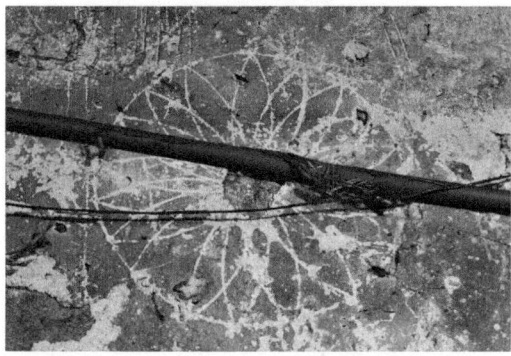

Fig. 5. One of many circular marks applied to the interior walls of a former threshing barn at Park Farm on the Chatsworth Estate.

Circular designs are

115

found in a number of locations with a preference for first-floor storage areas such as granaries and hay lofts. Here they can be found inscribed into the plaster or render, often in large numbers. Several variations on the typical designs could be applied in a single location. At Home Farm, Hassop the granary has a mass of intersecting, circular marks inscribed into a patch of surviving plaster.

Even when the interior walls are bare stonework, marks can be found on the timbers of roof trusses, or on internal doors and their frames. At Grindslow House in Edale a loft above a former cart shed has a number of circular marks boldly scribed onto the tie beams of its trusses. Other locations include stairwells, stables, and – as at Park Farm on the Chatsworth estate – the interior walls of former threshing barns.

Whilst most marks appear in buildings associated with the farmstead, they are also found in more isolated buildings. In the South West Peak there are several field barn cow houses, built in the nineteenth century, which have circular marks inscribed on their feed racks.

Burn marks

Flame-shaped burn marks are a well-known feature of early buildings and

Fig. 6. (top) Bold circular marks to a roof truss in a loft above a former cart shed, Grindslow House, Edale. These buildings underwent extensive renovation as the yard was developed in the 1880s.

Fig. 7. (middle) At Brushfield Hough near Taddington a number of the first floor storage areas have circular marks inscribed into the plaster. This range of buildings is thought to have been constructed in the first quarter of the nineteenth century. (Marks enhanced).

Fig. 8. (bottom) Circular marks to a hay cratch in a nineteenth-century field barn near Warslow, Staffordshire Moorlands. Mark a is also seen in a similar barn some four miles away, in the same location on the hayrack. (Marks enhanced).

it has been well established that they were deliberately made, with a key role played by the research of John Dean and Nick Hill in 2014.[9] There are various suggestions as to the purpose of these marks, including that they protected against fire and perhaps lightning.[10] But they have also been thought to be more generally protective, acting against malign influences and supernatural harm.[11] Dean and Hill date most burn mark activity between the late sixteenth and early eighteenth centuries.[12] However, burn marks have been recorded in later buildings; James Wright describes an example found on the timbers of an 1870s roof in the old laundry at Knole in Kent[13] and Edwards and Lake include them as potential finds in nineteenth-century farm buildings.[14] Burn marks in farm buildings are easily overlooked and probably occur far more widely than was thought.

They have been noted in a growing number of Peak farm buildings, both singularly and in small groups, in various locations. Often, like circular marks, they were made in and around first-floor storage areas. At One Ash Grange near Monyash, there is an obvious burn to the rear of the former granary door. A single burn is seen to a door frame in a hayloft, above the former stable at Poynton Cross farm, Windmill, while several other buildings have burn marks on the timbers of roof trusses. In some cases just a single burn has been applied to the tie beam of a truss.

Fig. 9. Burn mark to the rear of a granary door, One Ash Grange near Monyash.

Remembering the work of Ian Evans, who found burn marks on nineteenth-century stable partitions in Tasmania,[15] it seemed likely that similar examples might exist here in the Peak District. Now that the working horses are long gone, original stable partitions are rare, but a couple of extant examples show burn marks. In one case, where the stables date to 1850, burns were made to the kicking posts of partitions.[16] They have also been found on the backs of original stable doors.

Other examples appear to be associated with cattle. These include a small group of burns on a cow house door at Brushfield Hough, Taddington, and a

Fig. 10. Burn marks to a stable partition; the stables here are dated to 1850.

117

single burn mark at the feed passage entrance of an isolated cow house in the Edale valley.

Dating

There are obvious difficulties in dating marks and inscriptions on building fabric. Whilst both circular designs and burns feature in earlier Peak District farm buildings, there is no way of knowing at what point these marks were applied.[17] However, it is a little easier to date marks in later buildings. Historic maps and other records can help establish the construction date for a building which at least gives a terminus post quem for any inscribed marks.

Of the farm buildings in which marks have been recorded so far, most are of the nineteenth century; it is clear that the use of burns and circular marks continued until the end of the century at least, and quite possibly later. At Bubnell Farm, Bubnell, both types of mark were recorded on a pair of internal loft doors and their frames in a range of buildings extensively remodelled between 1879 and 1900.[18] It is very likely that these marks date from, or after, this rebuilding.

Fig. 11. Bubnell Farm, Bubnell. Burn marks and small circular marks to loft door and frame.

Fig. 12. Detail of circular mark from Fig. 11.

Some evidence and interpretation

Despite the widespread use into the late nineteenth century of both burns and inscribed circular designs, knowledge of these marks has all but gone from farming communities. Whilst both types of mark are currently considered to have had a protective function, we have virtually nothing in the way of documentary or anecdotal evidence, leaving us ignorant of the specific motivation for either type of mark. It is possible that on the farm, marks would have been made as a response to a variety of concerns. Recording physical evidence – the marks themselves and the places where they occur – becomes vital in working towards an understanding of how they were used.

Whilst circular designs and burns differ in appearance and method of application, and seldom appear together, it must be significant that they are found in the same locations. In particular, both forms of mark are found in and around haylofts and granaries.

Hay and processed grain stored in these areas would have been a valuable resource, essential for seeing a farm through the winter. It would have been important to keep them safe from harm, however caused.

Both burns and circular marks have been recorded on doors and door frames, with some circular marks found next to other openings such as taking-in doors and pitching holes. This could be seen as significant, again indicating that both kinds of mark may have had a protective role.

Easton suggests that it was tradesmen, such as those involved in the plastering of interior surfaces, who made the circular marks.[19] Examples recorded on hay racks, found in a pair of field barns in the Staffordshire Moorlands, suggest that joiners also inscribed their versions. Some four miles apart, the barns have identical forms of a circular mark positioned in a very similar location on each rack (see fig. 8). The same craftsman, or craftsmen, must have been involved in both barns. Both hayracks are very well made and of a similar construction; it could well be that the joiners fitted them and then finished the job by applying their circular designs.

As well as the protective role attributed in particular to circular marks, it has been suggested that those in later buildings may have been made for luck and good fortune. A paper on circular marks in a Devon threshing barn includes the view of a local agricultural contractor who knew the marks as 'harvest symbols', the intimation being they were made with an 'aspiration for fruitfulness' [20] This is an interesting view which is not easily dismissed.

The use of marks and symbols by tradesman and possibly farm workers to avert difficulties or in the hope of positive outcomes, would not be out of place, given the many well documented examples of how farming communities utilised 'common magic' at times of need.

The current view that marks in farm buildings warded against a variety of misfortune, does sit well when we consider the uncertainties of successfully raising livestock and producing crops. Events such as storms, drought, disease and fire could all bring adversity and financial disaster. Furthermore, the once widespread belief that valuable animals were vulnerable to bewitchment, and that some misfortunes were the result of malevolent activity, may play a part in explaining this practise.

Although the use of marks in farm buildings as discussed here, appears to be both a common and relatively recent practice, it is clear that many unanswered questions remain. It is hoped that continued recording here in the Peak District can make a contribution to the wider understanding of how these marks were used.

Acknowledgements
I am indebted to many farmers and building owners for allowing access and recording to take place. I would like to thank the following folks: Sandra Vickers, John Shirt, John Elliot, The Chatsworth Estate, The Peak District National Park Authority, Ed Warren, Bob and Judy Dilks, Henry Stephenson, Stephanie and Steven Wells, Dennis Collier and Tom Noel. Thanks also to David Orchard for mapping and Timothy Easton who has always been generous with knowledge and encouragement.

Notes
1. Timothy Easton, 'Like the circles that you find', *Society for the Protection of Ancient Buildings Magazine* (Winter 2015) pp.51–7 at p.54.
2. Bob Edwards and Jeremy Lake, *Peak District National Park Farmsteads Character Statement* (Peak District National Park Authority, 2017) p.1.
3. Edwards and Lake, *Farmsteads Character Statement* p.4.
4. Matthew Champion, *Medieval Graffiti: The Lost Voices of England's Churches* (London: Ebury, 2015) pp.31–44.
5. Timothy Easton, 'Apotropaic symbols and other measures', in *Physical Evidence for Ritual Acts, Sorcery and Witchcraft in Christian Britain: A Feeling for Magic*, ed. Ronald Hutton (Basingstoke: Palgrave Macmillan, 2016) pp.47–50; Brian Hoggard, *Magical House Protection: The Archaeology of Counter-Witchcraft* (New York: Berghahn, 2019) pp.74–86; Champion, *Medieval Graffiti* p.38.
6. Timothy Easton, 'Parallel worlds: barns and scribed circles', *Society for the Protection of Ancient Buildings Magazine* (Winter 2016) pp.42–9.
7. Matthew Champion, 'Graffiti Survey Record: The Stable Block, Belton House, Lincolnshire', unpublished report for the National Trust (2017) p.18, online at https://www.academia.edu/44821187/Graffiti_Survey_Record_The_Stable_Block_Belton_House_Lincolnshire_Client_National_Trust_2017 (accessed December 2021).
8. Tony Hack, 'The Bradford on Avon Monastic Barn: A Study and Interpretation of Apotropaic and Historic Graffiti' (2021), https://www.academia.edu/50402273/The_Bradford_on_Avon_Monastic_Barn_A_Study_and_Interpretation_of_Apotropaic_and_Historic_Graffiti (accessed December 2021).
9. John Dean and Nick Hill, 'Burn marks on buildings: accidental or deliberate?', *Vernacular Architecture* 45 (2014) pp1-15.
10. Easton, 'Apotropaic symbols and other measures' p.56.

11. Hoggard, *Magical House Protection* pp.95–6.
12. Dean and Hill, 'Burn marks on buildings' p.10.
13. James Wright, 'Mediaeval Myth Busting Blog #8: Burn Marks', 8th July 2021, https://triskeleheritage.triskelepublishing.com/mediaeval-mythbusting-blog-8-burn-marks/ (accessed December 2021).
14. Edwards and Lake, *Farmsteads Character Statement* p.78.
15. Ian Evans, 'Tasmanian Magic Research Project: Report of the second field season January 6th–27th 2018', https://www.academia.edu/36996265/Tasmanian_Magic_Research_Project_Second_Field_Season (accessed December 2021).
16. The owner of this building has requested that the location is not published.
17. For example, in 2016 I recorded a number of circular marks and burns marks on the trusses of the 1570s cruck barn at North Lees Hall, Hathersage.
18. Conference notes from a paper by Jeremy Lake at the Historic Farm Buildings Group Conference, the Peak District, 15th–16th September 2018.
19. Easton, 'Apotropaic symbols and other measures' p.61.
20. Laurie Smith, *Architectural Geometry: A Rare Geometrical Record From Devon* (Exeter: Historic Building Geometry, 2020) p.42.

Merels: Games, graffiti, symbols

Anthea Hawdon

Merels are a type of graffiti that take the form of old game boards. 'Merels' itself is another name for the game of Nine Men's Morris but it has become the generic term for this format of game, showing up in historic contexts as graffiti. There are four main board layouts that would be recognised as merels. (There are subtle variations that appear in the real-life examples, but they still fall under these four main types). These are Nine Men's Morris, Three Men's Morris, Nine Holes and Alquerque.

Three Men's Morris and Nine Holes are actually the same game but the board can be laid out with or without the interconnecting lines. Alquerque is more akin to draughts in the manner of play, which separates it from the true merels games. However, the design of the game board for alquerque shares enough similarities with the true merels boards to include it with them. All of these games were very popular at all levels of society during the Middle Ages with Nine Men's Morris and especially Three Men's Morris retaining that popularity into the early modern period and beyond.

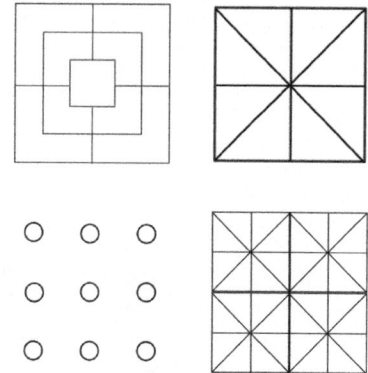

Fig. 1.(top left) Nine Men's Morris.
Fig. 2.(top right) Three Men's Morris.
Fig. 3. (bottom left) Nine Holes.
Fig. 4. (bottom right) Alquerque.

The game board designs appear as graffiti in many historic buildings, both secular and religious. There are many examples of them in cathedral cloisters and other areas of seating, where the boards appear scratched into the stonework. Here the assumption can be safely made that they were used for playing. The carving from Great Sampford church in Essex comes from an arcade in the chancel of the church where clerics would be seated.

Fig. 5. Great Sampford church, Essex.

However, and this is what makes merels relevant to building protection, there are also numerous examples of these game boards being found on a vertical surface where it would be impossible for them to be played. This is true of the Alquerque (Fig. 6) and Nine Men's Morris (Fig. 7) graffiti from Finchingfield church in Essex, and of the Nine Holes design from the Bradford-on-Avon Tithe Barn.

If the carved board game could not be used for actual play, then what is at work here? One possible explanation is in their locations. Two examples are in liminal spaces: the Nine Men's Morris and Alquerque board from Finchingfield church, which are in the window space and chancel arch, respectively. As for the Nine Holes graffiti, it is in a building chockful of protective designs such as daisy wheels.

Fig. 6. Finchingfield church, Essex.

These unplayable board games are found alongside other protective symbols and it can be surmised that they themselves had a protective or, at least, a symbolic role. What could that be?

The layout of the Nine Men's Morris board has the best claim to recognisable symbolism. It is related to the concept of the 'triple enclosure' in which a set of three concentric walls, each set with gates, encloses areas of great, greater and greatest holiness. The best example is Solomon's Temple as described in *Kings*, *Chronicles*, and especially *Ezekiel* chapter 40. Some manuscript illustrations of the Temple (both the earthly one and its heavenly counterpart) have a layout greatly resembling the Nine Men's Morris board.

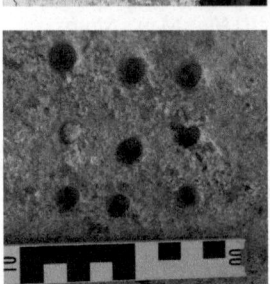

Fig. 7. (top) Finchingfield church, Essex.
Fig. 8. (bottom) Bradford on Avon Tithe Barn.

There is less documentary evidence to support this interpretation for the Alquerque and Three Men's Morris boards, but eight-armed cross symbols do appear. The baptismal cross has eight arms and fonts often have eight sides. There are also christograms that have an eight-armed format, such as the *Chrismon Sancti Ambrosii* at Milan Cathedral.

While there is little documentary evidence for the symbols behind the Three Men's Morris board, there is as yet none at all for Nine Holes. Having said that, three of anything in the context of a church generally has something to do with the Trinity. The Nine Holes board could be taken as the Trinity three times – the Trinity squared, if you like.

More study is needed in this area, especially of the Three Men's Morris board graffiti. But it could be we are seeing echoes and remnants of old protective symbols in these enigmatic inscriptions.

Fig. 9. Milan Cathedral.

Acknowledgements

Fig. 9 is from G. Dallorto (modified: D Bachmann), 2007, at https://commons.wikimedia.org/w/index.php?curid=50483677.

Notre Dame de Temniac: The landscape of a nineteenth-century altar back

Linda Wilson

History

The church of Notre-Dame de Temniac occupies a commanding position overlooking the beautiful medieval market town of Sarlat in the Dordogne region of France. Next to the church is a ruined castle, and the history of the church, the castle and the town are inextricably linked.

The known history of the church appears in a small book by L'Abbé G. Duverneuil, *Notre-Dame de Temniac, le chateau, l'église, le pèlerinage* (Perigueux, 1910), from which much of the historical information in this paper is derived.

The land on which the church stands was given to the abbey in Sarlat in 936 and in the sixth or seventh century a chapel was constructed, the first known religious building at Temniac. In 1153 the independent monastic estate of Sarlat, of which Temniac was a part, placed itself under the direct authority of the Pope. In 1318 the bishopric of Sarlat and the town became the seat of a new diocese created by Pope John XXII. The following year, the chapel at Temniac was reconstructed in the Byzantine style and Pope John XXII granted indulgences for visits there. During the Hundred Years' War (1337–1453), the neighbouring castle regularly changed hands between the French and the English, and the church is likely to have suffered in the conflict before its reconstruction in 1424.

The church and the castle suffered further depredation in the early stages of the Wars of Religion (1562–98) and were destroyed by the Protestants in 1562. The fate of the two continued to be joined at the hip, and both were reconstructed in 1593 by Monseigneur Louis de Salignac, the 27th bishop of Sarlat.

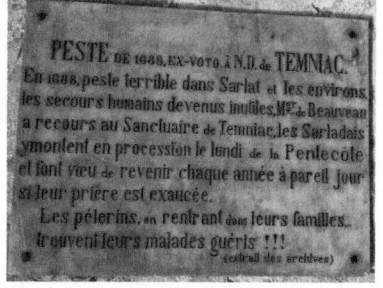

Fig.1. Plaque in the church commemorating the plague and the first miracle.

In 1627 the area was struck by a severe drought, and de Salignac organised a pilgrimage to Temniac by the White Penitents of Sarlat to pray for the aid of the Virgin Mary. A plaque in the church records that the pilgrims' wishes were granted the same day.

Calamity struck again in 1652 when the castle and the church were once more destroyed, this time by the army of Louis II de Bourbon, Prince of Condé. Ten years later, in 1662, the church was reconstructed by Monseigneur François de Salignac, and in 1671 the Sisters of Our Lady took refuge there.

As if this history of war and drought wasn't enough, a second plaque in the church states that in 1688 the area was struck by a devastating pestilence, probably an outbreak of bubonic plague. The people of Sarlat once again called on the Virgin Mary to aid them and Monsignor de Beauveau organised another pilgrimage up the hill to Temniac. The plaque states that when the pilgrims returned home, their loved ones had been cured. This is the second of the two miracles attributed to the Virgin Mary at Temniac. In thanks for this, the people of Sarlat fulfilled their vows by making an annual pilgrimage to the church.

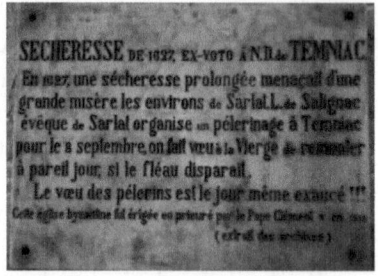

Fig.2. Plaque in the church commemorating the drought and the second miracle.

The church and the castle gradually fell into disrepair, despite the annual pilgrimages of the White Brotherhood and the Blue Brotherhood of Sarlat and in 1793, during the early years of the French Revolution, the church was looted and confiscated by the state, its archives lost or destroyed. In 1832, the church was reopened, now once again in the ownership of Sarlat, and 1856 saw its last major phase of reconstruction. Pilgrimages up the hill recommenced on the Monday of Pentecost and in the same year, on 8th September, the White Brotherhood again fulfilled the vows they took in 1627.

Notre Dame de Temniac in the 19th century

A plaque in the church commemorates the restoration work continued under the aegis of l'Abbé Manet, parish priest from 1885 to 1901. During the restoration, most of the plaster on the walls was stripped back to reveal the stonework underneath, displaying the characteristic honey-coloured local limestone, but losing any graffiti and other marks that might have existed on the plaster. The church owes much of its current, stark beauty to this renovation.

Fig. 3. Plaque in the church commemorating l'Abbé Manet, under whose aegis the church was restored in the nineteenth century.

Fig. 4. (left) Ex-voto plaques in crypt recording thanks for the fulfilment of prayers.
Fig. 5. (above left) Rosace design in pisé floor in centre of crypt.
Fig. 6. (above right) Notre-Dame de Temniac.

The crypt has no plaster and no informal marks on the walls. If any did exist, they have not survived the restoration. However, there is a wealth of *ex voto* plaques on the walls, placed there to record the fulfilment of pleas made to the Virgin Mary. The crypt also has a very fine *pisé* floor, made up of small, deep cobbles, with a flower petal design (known in France as a *rosace* and in Britain as a daisy wheel or hexafoil) providing decoration in the middle. The crypt also contains a simple modern stone altar and a statue of the Virgin Mary, recovered from the debris when the crypt was cleared as part of the restoration. The acoustics in the crypt are superb, and an interesting 'surround sound' effect can be obtained by standing on the *rosace* and speaking or singing.

The altar

The main area of interest for historical graffiti research is on the plaster of the altar back. The church was reopened for worship in 1832, so it is likely that the altar was installed then. At this time priests celebrated mass facing the altar, with their backs to the congregation.

Fig. 7. Altar.

On the plaster behind the altar is a wealth of handwritten prayers and pleas to the Virgin Mary, mainly written in pencil, but also scratched into the plaster. In addition there are names, dates and symbols including compass-drawn circles, a complete *rosace*, several pentagrams (sometimes alone, sometimes within a circle), an architectural sketch, what appear to be inscribed and drawn chairs, and even a piece of music.

The music graffito
The music graffito is 15cm long and 3cm high, evidently a chant. At first it seemed unlikely that this could be identified with any particular composition, but a lengthy research trail led to Christopher Hodkinson, Director of Music at Wyoming Catholic College in the United States, who recognised the notation as the first phrase of the Kyrie of Henri du Mont's *Messe Royale du premier ton*. The *Messe Royale*, which became very popular in France, was first published in 1669 and was republished in many chant books.[1]

Prayers and Dates
The prayers are mainly found on the back of the tabernacle, the box in the altar in which unused consecrated bread is stored, ready to be used again (it cannot simply be thrown away, since Christ is present in consecrated bread). The use of this most holy part of the altar for prayers to the Virgin Mary is unsurprising, as those seeking her aid would have been fully aware of the significance of the tabernacle. The practice of writing prayers on altar backs is well-attested in the area, as is their inscription on walls near the statues of popular saints; another example can be found in the abbey church of Saint Cyprien.

Fig. 8. (top) Altar back.
Fig. 9. (middle) Music graffito.
Fig. 10. (bottom) Graffiti on the back of the tabernacle.

Many of the prayers on the back of the tabernacle and elsewhere on the altar back are faint and difficult to read, but some are transcribed, with translations:

- *Sainte Vierge faites que mon grand père guerisse et je vous promets de venir toute la famille vous remercier* (Blessed Virgin, heal my grandfather and

I promise to come with all the family to thank you)
- *je vous prie de me conserver mes parents* (please I beg you to keep my parents)
- *MERE! Exauce ton enfant* (MOTHER! Hear your child) [illegible number] Mars 1954 [illegible number] March 1954)
- *Sauvez-le* (Save him)
- *Guerissez ma mère* (Heal my mother)
- *Notre Dame de* [illegible] *exaucez-nous je vous en conjure* (Our Lady of [illegible] hear us I beg you)
- *Vierge immaculée exauces mes prières* (Immaculate Virgin hear my prayers)
- *Oh Jesus! Oh Marie! Je vous confie tout tout! Je me fie à j'espère tout de vous. Merci! Merci! Merci!* [Oh Jesus! Oh Mary! I entrust everything to you! I trust in you. Thank you!]

Duverneuil, in the section *Inscriptions de demandes* of his chapter *La Vierge miraculeuse*, lists some of the requests made to the Virgin, using wording that corresponds (in some cases exactly, and elsewhere in summary) with the prayers found on the back of the altar, although Duverneuil does not say where he read these requests.[2] The lack of detail about location is an interesting omission in an otherwise detailed book, but the passage shows that the altar graffiti was known and found significant before 1910.

Whilst the pleas for aid do not, in general, have either names or dates attached to them, at the bottom of the tabernacle it is possible with some difficulty to read a few dates. The earliest is 7 September 1882 (*7bre* standing for *Septembre*). Others are 10 September 1889, 16 September 1899 and 20 September 1899. The similarity of the handwriting in each case leads to the conclusion that the dates were all written by the same person and might mark the dates of personal pilgrimages to the church, all clustered close to the 8th September, the festival of the Nativity of the Virgin Mary. There is also more recent graffiti, usually of the simple name and date type eg LUCY 1998, DAVID 1959, JACQUES 14-03-78, P.N. 99. The prayers were left by supplicants who did not see any need to add any identifying detail such as their names or even their initials to their pleas, or the date on which they were made, whereas other visitors to the church recorded their presence by means of their name or initials, often coupled with a date.

Other marks
Various symbols feature on the back of the altar, mainly inscribed in the soft plaster by a thin point, although some are more deeply scratched. These can

best be seen by the usual method of raking light from the side to cast shadows and improve definition. They include numerous small compass-drawn circles, pentagrams (both on their own and in circles), merels (a form of board game), a sketch that resembles the west wall of the church containing the main entrance, and even several chairs (three inscribed and one drawn in pencil; not something that has so far been found elsewhere in the region). The merels, common in the area, are the simple three men's morris form. Some merels, such as those in the cloisters of the cathedral of Saint Étienne in Cahors, are on horizontal surfaces and were almost certainly intended to be used to play the game, known as *jeu de moulin*. Others are on vertical surfaces, like those at Temniac, and the ones on the back of the choir stalls Abbey of Sainte-Marie in Souillac. These cannot have been used for game play and may well have some other significance, possibly apotropaic.[3]

The pentagram has been used to symbolise the five wounds of Christ (the connection with 'black magic' is entirely modern and would not have been in the mind of those inscribing them on the altar back). Pentagrams are commonly used as a mason's mark in both France and Britain: good examples can be found in the church of St Martin in Brive-la-Gaillard but they also appear in protective contexts.[4] At Temniac the pentagrams and geometric graffiti may be purely decorative, with no deeper meaning, but their placement on the back of an altar along with the *rosace* design makes some ritual significance more likely, despite the recent date of the altar. Even in the mid nineteenth century these symbols evidently persisted, either as apotropaic markings or as simple good luck charms.

The *rosace* appears in numerous contexts in the region: one can be found in the cathedral of Saint-Sacerdos in Sarlat, on the top of a misericord; there is a deeply inscribed partial *rosace* in the Chateau de l'Herm; three deeply carved designs of

Fig.11. Pentagram in compass drawn circle.

different types can be found over the doorway of a house on the main street in the small hilltop village of Beynac; and there is one on a stone roadside cross, bearing a worn date believed to be 1883, in the village of La Cassagne. The rose, like many other flowers, is associated with the Virgin Mary, and it is not surprising to find one in the restored crypt.

Use of the *rosace* for a floor decoration, as in the crypt at Temniac, is common in the Dordogne. Other fine examples can be found in the Chateau du Losse, the chapel of the Chateau de l'Herm, and the Chateau of Jumeillac. The design is also frequently found inscribed on both stone and wood: on the walls of the Maison Forte de Reignac; on the exterior of the church in Nadaillac; on the choir stalls of the abbey church of Sainte-Marie in Souillac and the Saint Sacerdos cathedral in Sarlat; and beside doorways on two old buildings in the village of Condat- sur-Vézère.[5]

Conclusion

The wealth of material on the altar back at Temniac will repay further detailed study. This note only scratches the surface – pun intended – of a rich landscape where the prayers on the back of the tabernacle sit above everything else, the jewel in a particularly impressive crown, while below them, spread out across the plastered surface, lie a rich array of symbols, names, dates and drawings, including an extremely rare example of a recognised musical notation. It is tempting to speculate that the latter was inscribed on the back of the altar as an *aide memoire* of a well-known composition that was, at some point, sung in the church.

The back of the altar has been used for three very different purposes over time, firstly as a vehicle for conveying and recording prayers to the Virgin Mary, secondly as an equally convenient surface for visitors to the church to record their presence, and thirdly as a place to make a wide variety of marks, some of which may have a significance beyond simple decoration or a means of whiling away time in a church. We can only guess at what was in the minds of those leaving the marks. The old adage that graffiti attracts graffiti may well have been at play here, but apart from the few dated examples of more modern name and date graffiti, the integrity of the early prayers and marks has largely been respected.

A photogrammetry survey of the altar back is intended, along with a more detailed comparison of the prayers and the ex-voto plaques, and further transcriptions of the faint handwriting. The intention is to record as much of the detail as possible for further research.

Acknowledgments

All photographs are by myself.

This work would not have been possible without the dedication of the people of Temniac who keep their beautiful church and its crypt in immaculate condition and open to visitors all year round during the hours of daylight. I would also like to thank the following: Stephen Dunn, John Challenger, Professor John Harper and Christopher Hodkinson for their help in identifying the music graffito; Marie-

Annick Mauroux for helping with the transcription of some of the prayers and Claude Lacombe for additional work on the altar back as well as for tracking down the book *Notre-Dame de Temniac, le chateau, l'église, le pèlerinage*, which helped enormously with this work; Anthea Hawdon for her love of graffiti and willingness to stand around in the cold for hours on end taking photographs and last, but very definitely not least, Graham Mullan for his hours of help with the production of the poster on which this paper is based.

Notes
1. Henri Du Mont, *Cinq messes en plain-chant, composées et dédiées aux révérends pères de la Mercy du Couvent de Paris* (Paris: R. Ballard, 1669).
2. G. Duverneuil, *Notre-Dame de Temniac, le chateau, l'église, le pèlerinage* (Perigueux: Cassard Freres 1910) pp.69–76.
3. See Anthea Hawdon, 'Merels: Games, Graffiti, Symbols' in this volume.
4. Matthew Champion, 'Magic on the walls: ritual protection marks in the medieval church' in *Physical Evidence for Ritual Acts, Sorcery and Witchcraft in Christian Britain: A Feeling for Magic* ed. Ronald Hutton (Basingstoke: Palgrave Macmillan, 2016) pp.19–28.
5. For discussion of this symbol and its possible apotropaic usage see Champion, 'Magic on the walls' and Timothy Easton. 'Apotropaic symbols and other measures for protecting buildings against misfortune' in *Physical Evidence* ed. Ronald Hutton pp.44–50.

About the authors

Brian Hoggard has been researching the archaeology of counter-witchcraft since 1999. Over that time he has collected and mapped thousands of examples, many of which are reported via his website www.apotropaios.co.uk. He has given talks and published widely, and is author or Magical Hour Protection – The Archaeology of Counter-Witchcraft (Berghahn, 2019).

Dr Debora Moretti, an archaeologist and historian, successfully completed her PhD in History at Bristol University in 2018. Her research was part of the Leverhulme Trust-funded project 'the Figure of the Witch' with Professor Ronald Hutton. Debora's Doctoral thesis examined the image of the witch and witchcraft in medieval and early modern Italy.

Debora's research interest covers the history of Italian and European magic and witchcraft in medieval and early modern period and also material evidence of magic in archaeological contexts. Her published research focuses on the interactions between magic, its archaeological evidence and the social perception of the historical practitioners of magic and witchcraft.

Jeremy Harte is a researcher into folklore and archaeology, with a particular interest in landscape legends and tales of encounters with other worlds. His latest book is Cloven Country: The Devil and the English Landscape, and previous works include the award-winning Explore Fairy Traditions, English Holy Wells and The Green Man. He is curator of Bourne Hall Museum in Surrey, and can be contacted at jrmharte@gmail.com.

Jeannine Woods lectures in the School of Languages, Literatures and Cultures in the University of Galway, Ireland. Her scholarly background encompasses the fields of Cultural Anthropology and Irish language, literature and ethnology. Her research interests include the themes of language, representation and identity in traditional and contemporary popular culture.

Linda Wilson is a retired solicitor with a lifelong interest in caves and caving. Her study of French cave art over a 25-year period gradually morphed into an interest in anything painted, engraved and written on cave walls, which has now extended to encompass protection marks, mason's marks, carpenter's marks and historic graffiti above and below ground. She is currently working on a project to record the graffiti in Kents Cavern, Torquay.

Her main research areas lie in both the UK and the Dordogne region of France.

Chris Wood researches, writes and talks on matters mythological and magical, applying his training as an environmental scientist to the intermingled worlds of history and legend. He also curates the Ickeny Collection (East Anglian Museum of Magic and Mythology: www.ickeny. co.uk) and helps organise Norwich Pagan Moot (www.norwichmoot.co.uk).

Jason Semmens, M.A., M.B.A., A.M.A., was born and brought up in West Cornwall and is currently the Director of the Museum of Military Medicine, near Aldershot. He is an independent scholar with research interests in the history of vernacular beliefs in the supernatural in the South West of England. He has published extensively, including articles in peer-reviewed journals and book compilations.

Marc Robben is a Belgian engineer-architect who has been researching masonry marks and other traces of superstition on buildings for many years. The research extends from Poland to England, from Sweden to Northern France. The results of that search can be found on the website: www.graafschaploon.be.

James Wright (Triskele Heritage) is a buildings archaeologist specialising in the mediaeval and early modern period. His PhD is on Tattershall Castle in Lincolnshire. He has an interest in the dynamic interaction between elite buildings and graffiti.

Andy Bentham has been recording mark making and older graffiti both independently and with groups such as the Derbyshire and Nottinghamshire Medieval Graffiti Survey, for the last decade. Living and working in the Peak District National Park has seen Andy focus his more recent recording in the buildings of working farms.

Anthea Hawdon is a co-founder of the Raking Light historic graffiti website. She enjoys searching for and recording historic graffiti anywhere she can find it, mostly in Essex. Her specialist subject within graffiti studies is those of merels and other game boards. Anthea has presented her work at conferences and gives regular talks to local history and church groups in the south-east.

Index

Abbey of Sainte-Marie in Souillac 132-3
Acallam na Senórach 36
Agincourt 25
Alchemist's Room 64
All Saints Hawton, Nottinghamshire 107
Alphamstone, Essex 63
Alquerque 123-4
Alveley, Shropshire 30, 35
ampullae 105
Anderton, Lancashire 63
Anglo-Scandinavian Cross 73
Appleton Wiske, Yorkshire 29
Aran jumper 49
Archaeology of Ritual and Magic 15
Armagh, Northern Ireland 9
Armitage, Natalie 13
Arundel Castle, West Sussex 105
Ash Grange, Monyash 117
Ashmolean Museum, Oxford 18
Ashprington, Devon 26, 29
Asia 49
Aston-upon-Trent, Derbyshire 26
Atkinson, Canon J.C. 72
auseklis cross 64-5

Bagworth, Leicestershire 105
Baines, William 63
Baring-Gould, Sabine 58, 66
Barnet, Battle of 36
Barr-Taylor, Kati 66
Barrett, W.H. 8-9
Barrow, Shropshire 35
Barton-in-Fabis, Nottinghamshire 31
Bath 43
bats' wings 87
Battle of Magh Leana 36
Bealtaine 44

Beetham, Westmoreland 31
Benthall Hall, Shropshire 77
Berkeley Castle 59
Berlin 36
Berwick, Sussex 30
Bethu Brigte 44
Bever, Edward 15
Beynac 132
Biddy 41, 46, 50, 51
Billingsley, John 3, 31, 37, 66
Birmingham 25
Bishop Mel 44
Black Dog 87
Blight, Thomasine 87
Bodiam Castle 102
Bogha Bríde 48
bone scoops 69, 75, 76, 79
Bonser, Wilfrid 32
Book of Invasions, The 42
Black Horse Drove 8
Bradford on Avon 115, 124
Brasenose Lane, Oxford 70
Brassicaceae 89
Brat Bríde 41, 45, 47
Brídeog 41, 46, 50, 51
Brigantia 42
Brigid's Belt 41, 50, 52
Brigid's Bow 48
Brigid's Cloak 41, 45, 47
Brigid's Cross 41, 43, 46, 48, 49, 50, 54
British 17
Broicseach 42
Browne, Sir Thomas 78
Broughton, Lincolnshire 26, 30
brúitín 46
Brushfield Hough near Taddington 114, 117
Bryant Homestead, South Deerfield,

137

Mass. 9
Bubnell Farm, Bubnell 118
Buchan, John 32
Buckden Palace, Lincolnshire 108
Building Magic: Ritual and Re-Enchantment in Post-Medieval Structures 21
Burgundy Cross 77
burn marks 113-4, 116-9
Burton Hastings, Warwickshire 29
butterfly cross 76, 78

Cahokia Courthouse 7
Callington, Cornwall 85, 87
Cambourne, Cornwall 86
Cambrensis, Giraldus 43
Cambridgeshire Customs and Folklore 8
Carpaccio, Vittore 105
Castle Acre, Norfolk 101
Cathedral of Saint-Sacerdos, Sarlat 132
Celtic cross 73
Chalain-le-Comtal, Loire 95
Challenger, John 133
Champion, Matthew 65, 106
Chartered Institute for Archaeologists 20
Chatres Cathedral 90
Checkley, Staffordshire 27, 30
Chedzoy, Somerset 36
Cheshire 10, 25-6,
Chester 3, 26, 66
Chi Rho monogram 74, 77
Chrismon Sancti Ambrosii, Milan Cathedral 124
Christchurch Priory 107
chrysoms 77
Cill Dara, 'church of the oak' 43
Cill Ghobnait, Co. Kerry 51
circles, inscribed 64-5, 103, 113-6, 118-9, 129

Cliffoney, Co. Sligo 48
Cloch na mBorradh, Sixmilebridge, Co. Clare 36
Cloch na nArm 37
Clun, Shropshire 31
Cogitosus 42
Colchester Castle, Essex 105
Collier, Dennis 120
Commarque, Sauveboeuf 57
Condat- sur-Vézère 133
Conyers 7
Cor Deiseal 46
Corinium Museum, Cirencester 63
Cornish Gorsedd 86
Cornish Museum, West Looe, Cornwall 88
Cormac's Glossary 42-3
Coscrach na Cét. Leinster 36
Crail, Fife 32
Crecy 25
Crios Bríde 41, 52
Crockets 91
Cromwell 35
Cromwell, Ralph Lord 102, 105, 108
Cros Bhríde 41, 48
cross-flowers 89, 90, 92
Cruciferae 89
Crumlin, Co. Galway 50, 52
Culloden 35

Dachplatte 94
Dagaz rune 76, 78, 79
Dagda 42
Daisy wheel 65, 104, 124
daoini maithe 53
Davies, Owen 21
de Bonaventure, Léopold 64
de Honnecourt, Villard 91
de Roos, William 105
de Strelley, Sir Sampson 101
Dean, John 117

decussata 76, 77
Derbyshire 26, 29
Devon 26-7, 29, 34
Dilks, Bob and Judy 120
Dirleton Castle, Scotland 31
Discovery of Witchcraft 87
Dixon, Philip 101
Donar 93
Donegal 54
Dordogne 57
Douai University 73
Doune Castle, Scotland 31
dragon 25
Dragon Hall, Norwich 102
Druids 53
Duke of Burgundy 77
Duke of Cumberland 35
Dunlichty, Inverness-shire 27
Dunn, Stephen 133
Dunton Bassett, Leicestershire 30, 32, 35
Durham 7
Duverneuil, L'Abbé G. 127, 131

Easton, Timothy 70, 106, 113, 115, 119, 120
Edward III 25
Edward the Confessor 101
Egmond, Shropshire 35
Egypt 32
elixir of immortality 64
Elliot, John 120
Ellis, Bryn 9
Elsdon, Northumberland 6
English Americans 7
Essex 31, 63
Ethelbert Gate, Norwich Cathedral 105
Eton College 108
Etruscan 17
Europe 5, 18, 41, 49

Evans, Ian 117
evergreen house garlic 93
Exeter Cathedral 104

fairies 25, 53
Feast of St Brigid 41
Felsted, Essex 31
Fian Mac Cumhall 36
Fianna 36
Fife 27
Finchingfield church, Essex 124
Finland 7-8
Fitstziegel 94
five wounds of Christ 74, 77, 103, 132
Foley, Rocky & Kathy 9
Folklore Society, The 3
Ford, Joseph 72-3, 74
foundation sacrifice 5, 8
Fourknocks 49
France 36
French Revolution 128
French settlers 7

Gaeltacht communities 41
Gaul 41
geansaí Árann 49
Geasa Draoidecht 53
Geddes, Jane 70, 77
Germany 33, 34, 73, 94, 97
Ghent 94
Gilchrist, Roberta 16
Gill, Harry 34, 36
Gimbutas, Marija 41. 49
Glas Gaibhnenn 43
Gloucestershire 37
Goibniu 43
Gothic 89-92
Gorumna Island, Co. Galway 49
Grabenstetten, Germany 71
Graebe, Martin 66
Grassmayrmuseum, Innsbruck 95

Great Sampford church, Essex 123
Great Urswick, Lancashire 29
Grimoire 79
Grindslow House, Edale 116
Gyfu rune 76, 79, 80
Gypsy 33

Haddon Hall, Derbyshire 105, 107
Halkyn Mountain Communities in Times Past 9
Hall, Linda 70
Hallowe'en 44-5
Halton East, North Yorkshire 7
Harper, Professor John 133
Harte, Jeremy 66
Hastings, William Lord 108
Hawdon, Anthea 66, 134
Heck Posts 71, 74, 79
Henry VII 101
Henry VIII 95
Hertfordshire 10
Hester, Owen 53, 54
Hidden Charms conference 3, 26, 66, 85
High Cross of Moone, Co. Kildare 49
Hill, Nick 117
Historic England 20
Hobby-horse 10
Hodkinson, Christopher 133
Hoggard, Brian 16, 21, 37, 66, 80
Holme Pierrepont Hall, Nottinghamshire 105-6
Holy Rood Buckland Newton, Dorset 107
Holy Trinity Blythburgh, Suffolk 106
Holy Trinity, Hull 104
Holy Trinity Tattershall, Lincolnshire 103, 105
Home Farm, Hassop 116
Hooden horse 5, 10
Hoodoo 78

house garlic 93
Hornby Castle, Wensleydale 7
horseshoes 5, 10
Houlbrook, Ceri 13, 21
Hukantaival, Sonja 7
Hulubas, Adina 9
Hundred Years War 28, 127
Hunt, Rober 85
Hutton, Ronald 17
Hutton-le-Hole 72

Iceland 79
Ickeny Collection 75
IHS 64
Imbolc 4
Inguz 79
Ireland, Rebecca 66
iris flower 93
Irish Folklore Commission 41
iron 10
Isle of Man 7
Italy 17-18

Jacobites 35
Jarrot Mansion 7
Jeffries, Nigel (MOLA) 21
Jesus 73
Johnson, Matthew 102
Judaism 62, 104
Jumeillac 57
Jupiter's beard 93

Kannebakkersland, Germany 94
Kenilworth, Warwickshire 32, 102
Kent 10
Kenton, Devon 29, 32
Kibworth Harcourt Windmill, Leicestershire 106
Kildare, Ireland 43, 49
Killaloe 49
Kirby Muxloe Castle, Leicestershire

108
Knole, Kent 117
Knouchley Farm, Calver 113
Knowth 49

Lá Fhéile Bríde 41
la joubarbe 93
Lacombe, Claude 66, 134
Lambley, Nottinghamshire 29
Landesmuseum Württemberg 71
Laon, Cathedral of 90
Lascaux 57
laying the witch 72
Lebor Gabála Érenn 42
Leland, Charles 32
lightning 93
Limburg, Belgium 96
Lincoln 27, 106
Liscannor, Co. Clare 52, 53-4
Longnor, Staffordshire Moorlands 114
Louis II de Bourbon, Prince of Condé 128
Lúnasa 44, 53
Lygan y Wern, Halkyn 9
Lyme 27

MacCana 42
Maerlant, Jocob 91
Magic, Ritual and Witchcraft 15
Magical House Protection: The Archaeology of Counter-Witchcraft 21
Manchester Museum 63
Maremma, Tuscany 18
Mari Lwyd 5, 10, 11
Marian mark 61, 103, 106, 109
Marktkirche, Hannover 104
Martainville Castle, Eure, Normandy 92
Mary Rose 28
Matthews, Rubyna 7
Mauroux, Marie-Annick 133-4
Mayfield, Sussex 32

Medieval Life 16
memento mori 3
merels 123
mermaid 3
Merrifield, Ralph 15-16, 18, 21
mesh marks 79
Middlesex 36
Middleton, Warwickshire 29
Milan Cathedral 125
Mitchell, Stephen 79
Mithraism 62
Monmouth Rising 36
Monsignor de Beauveau 128
Monseigneur François de Salignac 128
Monseigneur Louis de Salignac 127
Mór, Eoghan 36
Mugginton, Derbyshire 29
Mullan, Graham 66, 134

National Centre for Early Music 4
National Folklore Collection 41
Naunton Beauchamp, Worcestershire 29, 32
Nauthiz 79
Neolithic chalk cylinders 76
Netherlands 34, 73
Nevilles 7
Newark 102-3
Newgrange 49
Nine Men's Morris 123-4
Nine Holes 123-4
Noel, Tom 120
Norse charm inscriptions 79
Notre-Dame de Paris 90
Notre-Dame de Temniac, le chateau, l'église, le pèlerinage 127
Notre-Dame de Temniac, Sarlat, Dorogne 127, 129
North Hill, Cornwall 86
Northern Ireland 9
Northumberland 7, 36

141

Ó Catháin, Séamas 46, 51, 52
Ó Duinn, Seán 43
Ó Súilleabháin, Sean 5
Oakley, Robin 7
Odal / Othala rune 79
Offchurch, Warwickshire 29
Oíche Shamhna 44, 50
Old Cornwall movement 85, 88
Old White Hart, Newark, Nottinghamshire 102-3
Open Air Museum, Bokrijk, Limburg 93
Orchard, David 120
Order of St Patrick 77

Packwood, Warwickshire 30
Paignton, Devon 30, 34
Park Farm, Chatsworth Estate 115
PATERNOSTER 63
Paynter, William Henry 85
Peak District 113
Peak District National Park Authority 120
Peebles, Scotland 27
pentagram 103-4, 106, 129, 132
perpetual fire 43
Physical Evidence for Ritual Acts 17
Pinnacles 91-2
Pitt-Rivers Museum, Oxford 72
Poitiers 25
Pompeii 62
Pope John IV 95
Pope John XXII 127
Popular Romances of the West of England 85
Portable Antiquities Scheme 105
Porter, Enid 8
Portmarnock, Ireland 7
Postgate, Father Nicholas 73
poundies 46
Poynton Cross farm, Windmill 117
Price, Harry 87

Pystry, Whyler 85-6

Quickwell Hill, St David's 7
quincunx 77-8
Quintinus 96

Raidió Éireann 48
Raking Light 3
Ralph's Cross 74
Realities of Witchcraft and Popular Magic in Early Modern Europe 15
Reims Cathedral 91
Renfrew, Colin 14
Rhea, Nicholas 72-3
Riche Chapel, Felsted, Essex 31
Rilla Mill, Cornwall 87
Rivington, Lancashire 63
Robben, Marc 69
Roc de Cazelle, Beaune valley 57
Rockingham Castle, Northamptonshire 105
Rohan Hours 92
Roman 17, 62
Romanesque 69, 89, 91
Roman Inquisition 18
Romanian Academy 9
Römerturm, Cologne 98
rosace 59-60, 129, 132
rosettes 98, 105-7, 115
Ros Muc, Co. Galway 52
ROTAS 62
Roussot, Alain 64
Roussout-Laroque 58-9
runes 76, 78, 79
Russia 5, 9
Ryedale Folk Museum 72

Saint Cyprien, abbey church of 130
Saintes-Maries pilgrimage 33
Saint-Remi of Reims 90
Saint Symphorien chapel, Château de

Boussargues 98
saltire cross 77
Samain 37
Samhain 44
Sandklef, Albert 5
Sanas Cormaic 42
SATOR 62, 63, 65
Savigny, Rhone 95
Scandinavia 5, 9
Scot, Reginald 87
Scotland 27, 31, 32, 77
Sedgemoor 36
Sedum majus 93
Semmens, Jason 85
Sempervivum tectorum 93
Shirt, John 120
Shotwick, Cheshire 25-6, 29, 35
Shrawley, Worcestershire 29
Sisters of Our Lady 128
Sir Gawain and the Green Knight 103
Sixmilebridge, Co. Clare 36
Soissons, Cathedral of 90
solar motifs 98
Solihull 31, 33
Solomon 104
Solomon's Temple 124
Spellbound 18-19
Spiegel Historiael 91
Spooner, Barbera C 86
Squeen Lodge, Ballaugh, Isle of Man 7
Stafford-King, Nathan 80
Stang End, Danby 72
Star of David 78
Staunton-on-Wye, Herefordshire 5-6
Stephenson, Henry 120
stiepeltekens 73, 80
Stirling Castle, Scotland 31
Stobo Kirk, Peebles, Scotland 27, 32
Stoke Golding, Leicestershire 29-30
Stokeingteignhead, Devon 29, 30
Stone of the Sword 37

Strelley, Nottinghamshire 101
St Albans Abbey 106
St Andrew's Bredwardine, Herefordshire 104
St Botolph's Trunch, Norfolk 106
St Brigid's Day 41, 44
St Brigid's Well. Cliffoney, Co. Sligo 48
St Brigid's Well, Liscannor, Co. Clare 52, 53-4
St Davids, Pembrokeshire 7
St Edburgha's, Yardley, Warks 26
St Helen, Norwich 70
St James Aslackby, Lincolnshire 103
St John Maddermarket, Norwich 70
St Leonard's Scarcliffe, Derbyshire 104
St Margaret of Antioch, Cley-next-the-Sea, Norfolk 71
St Martin in Brive-la-Gaillard 132
St Martin's Fincham, Norfolk 106
St Mary and All Saints Fotheringhay, Northamptonshire 107
St Mary and All Saints Hawksworth, Nottinghamshire 104
St Mary and All Saints Sculthorpe, Norfolk 105
St Mary's Bottesford, Leicestershire 105
St Mary's Cheltenham, Gloucestershire 105
St Mary's Creative Space, Chester 3
St Mary's Happisburgh, Norfolk 105
St Mary's Lowdham, Nottinghamshire 106
St Mary's Troston, Suffolk 103
St Michael and All Angels, Ledbury, Herefordshire 71
St Michael Landrake, Cornwall 105
St Michael monogram 78-9, 80
St Michael's, Shotwick, Cheshire 25
St Nicholas Sevenoaks, Kent 106
St Nonna Altarnum, Cornwall 105

St Patrick 77
St Peter and St Paul Fakenham, Norfolk 106-7
St Petersberg 9
St Wilfrid's Kelham, Nottinghamshire 105
Suckley, Worcestershire 31
Sulis-Minerva 43
swastika 48
Sweden 5
sweordes stān 37
Swynnerton, Staffordshire 34

Tasmania 117
Tattershall Castle, Lincolnshire 92, 101-2, 107-8
The Making of the Human Mind 14
Theoretical Archaeology Group 13
Thirsk, North Riding of Yorkshire 26, 29
Thorpe, Derbyshire 29
Three Men's Morris 123-5
threshold 42, 45. 46
thunderblade 93
Thuxton, Norfolk 7
Topographia Hibernica 43
Totnes, Devon 26, 28
Touron, Jean-Max 64, 66
Towards an Archaeology of the Mind 14
triskele 48
Tuatha Dé Danann 42
Tudor House Museum, Southampton 70, 80
Turner, Victor 50

University of Bristol 17
University of Liverpool 13
University of Machester 13
USA 5, 7, 69
Van Gennep, Arnold 50

Vézère valley 57-8
Vickers, Sandra 120
Viollet-le-Duc 94

Wales 8-9, 10, 11
Walker, Peter 72
Warren, Ed 120
Wars of the Roses 36
Wars of Religion 127
Warslow, Staffordshire Moorlands 116
Watton, East Yorkshire 105, 107
Weber, Max 88
Weddinton Castle 28, 30
Wells, Stephanie and Steven 120
Welsh love spoon 75
Weserraum 98
Westbury on Trym, Gloucestershire 37
Westminster, Abbey and Palace 101
Westwood, Jennifer 28
Whetstone, Friern Barnet, Middlesex 36
Whetstone, Leicestershire 29
White Penitents of Sarlat 127
Wilford, Nottinghamshire 30
Wiliam, Eurwyn 8
Winceby Stone 36
Winchester 102
Witchcraft and Folklore of Cornwall, The 85, 88
witch-posts 69, 71
Wooler, Northumberland 36
Wright, James 27, 117

Yardley, Warwickshire 25, 29, 32-3
yellow iris 93
York 3, 106
Young Knight in a Landscape 105

Zonhoven, Limburg, België 95